AF077638

MAMMON
A CHRONICLE OF OBSERVANCES
Jerusalem 1130 A.D.

MAMMON

Copyright © 2024 Redmond Holt

Paperback ISBN: 978-1-915223-35-7

All rights reserved.

No part of this publication may be reproduced, stored in a retrieval system, or transmitted in any form or by any means, electronic, mechanical, photocopying or otherwise, without prior written consent of the publisher except as provided under United Kingdom copyright law. Short extracts may be used for review purposes with credits given.

Except in the case of historical fact, any resemblance to actual persons living or dead is purely coincidental.

Published by

Maurice Wylie Media
Your Inspirational & Christian Book Publisher

For more information visit
www.MauriceWylieMedia.com

Dedication

To my two sons; Luke and James.
Thank you for blessing my life.

Contents

Exordium 13

Part 1: Fullest of spate 17

Part 2: Beyond the consequence of fear 33

Part 3: Skulk ye devils the darkened halls 49

Part 4: Plough the horizon 65

Part 5: Jerusalem 81

Part 6: The seed of historie future 97

Convergence 113

Addendum 129

Exordium

**To his Most Excellent Majesty, Henry the First,
King of England and Duke of Normandy.**

May it please Your Majesty, Herein, scratched and compiled, these parchment mumblings capture a forthright endeavour to faithfully report upon the undertaking of your Royal Commission by Earl Uxbury to Jerusalem in the year of Our Lord, 1130AD. As advised both the compass of Uxbury's current orientation and the location of acquired bounty remain unclear at the time of this impartation.

As previously requested by His Highness I attach the diary of he whom we called Jonah; the stem of his observances unfolds the catalogue of our tale to fullest release.

Knew we not this sun, salt sea blasted Jonah. He blistered and fatigued, plank rescued from some forsaken Mediterranean position off the south coast of the Kingdom of Frankia. O'er time exposed he our vice; our vilest intentions. Made he us consider our colluded paths, many indeed considering eternity, be it for some for the very first time.

Belonged he nowhere, yea concomitantly everywhere. Oft despised where he lay his head, he was no man and yet everyman. He expressed varying degrees of disposition, conveying demonstrably both the ease and discomfort of the fragile human condition. He, Jonah, became to us an enigma; troubling and beguiling each encountered soul in equal measure.

At times desired we his death; his demise. Our plotted thoughts collectively singular; orchestrating manoeuvres toward his malfeasance. Yet Uxbury trusted this Jonah though irked this stranger Rome's pretender popes and laud of crusade gathered princes on more distant foreign shores.

He was but a simple man. Knowest we not at even this stage his name. His heritage, despite investigation, remains obtuse. Carried he no longer title or baggage; he devoid of all earthly encumbrances as if this world nare longer composed his predominant concern. Despite all he became my friend.

Christened we he Jonah; birthed he within us each our consciences.

I remain,

Bozeman Edwards,
Secretary (former) to the Earl of Uxbury.

A private diary of he who they called Jonah

A CHRONICLE OF OBSERVANCES

Part 1

Fullest of Spate

Fathom stretch of salt sea swirl,
a roiling tempest be the very heart of man.

FULLEST OF SPATE

I

Draped o'er Pythagorean lines,
celestial charts hued by faint lantern light,
the olde mariner traced the course of star
with measuring strings attached to briar,
searching... marking... recording notes
on yellowed parchment, corners creased,
then catching quick the Captain's eye
signalled too soon mine time to die.

II

The mariner through darkness timed the moon,
counting slow the cumulus swoon,
battered at times by storm flung wave,
he deftly sought mine dark depth grave.
Caped in wool hood clasped close to shield
the Captain surveyed the tempest seas,
midst heaving deck and creaking hull
held he in check the choler for cull.

III

With nod imperceptible he turned his crew,
my fate now sealed, last breaths I drew,
"Crucify him! Crucify him!" screamed they mine maim,
their blood lust fraught, mine cruor to drain.
"Hoist him up yon joist wood high!"
"Shroud his corpse in blood drench sail!"
Their cries mine ears no longer heard,
I readied now for assaults last charge.

IV

Captain's countenance fierce and manner gruff,
with scarred cheek and bristles rough,
this anointed leader of a lost host of men
played the role of sovereign king.
Whilst using his bulk to intimidate
he observed me close and cursed mine faith
then standing back so all could hear
composed his speech with theatrical flair.

V

"It hast been mine pleasure this one score year
to lead these fellows through war and cheer,
responsibility mine their work and keep
to busy at port this trading ship.
If called upon I judge affairs
with jurisprudence moderately fair,
mine crew you've rattled to deepest core
and brought each man to the extremity of woe."

VI

"Pirates, brigands, cut-throats we
confined to roam the plunge black sea,
murderers, vilest in our midst,
desire they thine death aboard mine ship.
The charge, you too holy for any one man,
too honest to engage in nefarious plan,
too meek and mild and full His Word,
enough they say of you we've heard."

VII

This was no legal ministering court,
the Captain no Emperor of Rome's consort,
he readied, steadied, subdued the crowd,
discharging verdict with no form record.
"I charge thee fellow!" he expressed with rage
with thunderous roar from his Mediterranean stage,
"We told you leave your Christ at port!
We ought hurl thee quick from our ark of float!"

VIII

I had been confined to rust wrapt cage,
imprisoning bars neath full chested sails,
unchained, unfettered now midst night of dark
I arose to address from plinth wood bark.
Marauders they together with calamitous desire
ignited within me a righteous fire,
I pelt with rain and stinging bruise,
skin purple raw and by angers mist roused.

IX

With clubs in hands and burnished sticks,
the desperate rabble stood mid-ship,
silent a time, they force drew breath,
stood to listen to mine address,
hair thin triggers stretched to coil,
I knew I possessed but little time
and drawing lung of salty air
stood forward... paused... said silent prayer.

X

A dangerous mob needs just one spark
to blow a barrel casket high,
I stood, observed the sailor crew,
discerned the mood, their attention drew.
"Six months I worked this agitated deck.
Six months I encouraged with every breath.
Six long months ye anathematized under influence o gin.
Six! Six! Six! Ye devils grim."

XI

"Brood o vipers, ye charlatan horde,
I stand afore ye bloody gored,
ye murderers, ye killers, consumed by vice,
hostages to yer fortunes and crime's delight,
I pointed all to God's love bright,
to His Son Christ Jesus who died yer death,
ye guilty butchers, lying tongues and eyes,
bow ye... kneel... claim repentance's prize."

XII

Some say I a fool, methinks me not,
some say I should have forgiven their decaying rot,
but that time I spoke I feared no dread,
they already committed to mine soon death.
The Captain fought to retain control
but then subscribed to excites explode,
he also fearful on consideration I suppose
lest he too be flung from the ships wild roll.

XIII

Mayhem released under the Creator's moon,
no shade in the shadow that announced my doom,
clubs and blows with sting of whips
bit my skin and force tore strips,
metal bits and cleft of nail,
unleashed my blood beneath the sails,
shouts and roars and drenching spit;
devils from hell from abaddon's pit.

XIV

All time stopped, all noise went quiet,
vowed I to unconsciousness mine non-comply,
then lifted high to pall-bear embrace,
I watched detached, each step haze traced.
The Captain caught mine half closed eye,
loosed mockers taunt then waved goodbye
and signalling consent by drawn sword
catapulted they mine tired bones o'erboard.

XV

Flail of arms, wild reckless limbs,
obscured in pitch o'er freezing seas,
long drop shadow o'er protecting rails,
ditched o'erboard, tossed to waves.
Seemed like forever, no harmony in sway,
absconds dance from maddened fray,
perfect silence then salt water gasp,
mine ocean crypt disclosed at last!

XVI

The rush of water awoke mine mind,
thoughts alighted to more recent times,
six months contained on that crate of boards,
surviving midst a brooding horde.
Cavalier brigands off Alkebulan's west coast,
brutish hunts for chattel and gold,
captured they, shipped they many men;
trading flesh fore voyaging again.

XVII

Murderous journeys their gruesome trade,
through lush green forests and gold sand glade,
innocents stalked then set 'pon,
wrenched from family roots generations long.
Poor souls were thrown to heave of hold,
water and bread flung to their dark abode,
they fought and clamoured for sustenance's prize,
the strongest succeeded whilst the weakened died.

XVIII

The crew hedged bets on every vice,
which human would live and which wretch would die,
quick to cheat at play of cards,
knives at the ready to cut and carve.
Pretended they all they bosom mates,
but each too well acquainted with blood lust hate,
collected together from corners far flung,
only the Captains threats quieted each one.

XIX

I fear such the way with bawdy men,
one second at peace the next plotting gain,
made it mine ministry to take a stand,
preached on Sabbaths The Lord's gracious plan.
Salvation by grace, free to all,
a change of heart promised to live life to the full,
urged I repentance, looked each square in the eyes,
but subjected they me to loathes despise.

XX

Continued I The Lord's mission to plot
from Jack frost morn till the sun's night drop,
aroused them, galvanised them toward one intent:
their souls to save, for each repent!
Yea alas they a maddened fire,
aggravated all, provoked to ire,
mine entreaties angered and slow brewed their blood,
hence mine predicament! They'd had enough.

XXI

This was no baptism but cruel callous death,
submerged I whole in hades depth,
sinking further down below
a look upward purchased no faint light glow.
This is it thought mine mind,
steadied mine nerve in darkened bind,
soon mine Saviour in Heaven's light,
an end I hoped to sin's poisonous bite.

XXII

Neighbour to the reaper at lungs protest
then Christ's miracle occurred, mine cadaver's release,
mine plea to throne-room securely heard,
resurrections bounty; mine circumstances transferred.
Charged I one last barrage to air,
popped like a cork from neptune's false lair,
all strength exhausted I flailed and gasped,
escaped from death; secured one last chance.

XXIII

The olde mariner salt had deliberated well
for they deposited I in a far flung hell,
caught faint lantern glimmer from my half bruised eye
whilst tall ships shadow away didst glide.
I bereft but alive in this isolated stretch,
desolate, alone, a poor rat sodden wretch,
but then captured from ship a faint shadow glance;
something o'erboard in drop plummet dance.

XXIV

Forced I a swim through sea wild breeze,
limbs tired... slow... found rhythms release,
I floundered, struggled but with determined grit
pursued I the chart of disappearing ship.
Then at last with swims lunged attack
mine arm struck gold! A full length plank!
Not embarrassed to say as I climbed aboard
mine tears didst abound to fresh o'erflow.

XXV

Then a thunderous furious storm eruption,
avalanched lightening midst drumming distortion,
suspended waves framed furlong thick
submerged to caverns obsidian bleak.
Stretched I out long like a corpse wrought tight,
satan's tentacles, his lunge deep smite,
to the bowels of the crust mine plank I sailed,
wrestling like Jacob against hellish assail.

XXVI

No expectation but peak and trough,
no sight, no horizon, just sudden drops,
spinning, twisting, roaring blind,
rage topped waves white cliff high.
With breath laboured and anguished brow,
face clenched tight, mine hands clasped bough,
I prayed The Lord mine soul to keep,
He to shelter me from the devils reach.

XXVII

Possessed I nothing but looming dread
then knocked out cold, mine plank mine bed,
unconscious for hours so it seemed
I awoke to faint light and calmer seas.
I observed natures elements begin their improve
yet spent most that day fraid to move,
with no land in sight I found depressions despair
and sat on mine plank in confusions trance stare.

XXVIII

Second lights clock arrived seasons too soon,
I exhausted, deflated atop precious boom,
emotional carnage swept through mine brain
as idol poseidon beckoned from lost mariner's grave.
Some sharks slunk by with menace of fin,
a dolphin edged closer with his chattering grin,
a mackerel jumped to land on my floating tree,
Salvations mercy! Yahweh's manna for me.

XXIX

Secured and encased in The Lord's love bright,
started the day to draw the third night,
those hours wrapt in splendours star flung surprise;
the cosmos entire exploded in light.
Constellations and planets in full circle engage,
harkened Abraham from memorised page,
as many the stars of the night wide stretch sky,
displayed He His Majesty, I blessed from on High.

XXX

Sealed by His Spirit from mine float embarkation,
I was commissioned in weakness; His strength to extol.
Inward conviction, His death and resurrection,
His call on mine life; His righteousness unfurled.
The veil of mine understanding rent all asunder,
the sins of nation's leaders I steel charged to expose.
No visit of Gabriel angel but akin Zacharias,
this revelation of mission I too wondered – How?

XXXI

The third day drew breath, this journey unceasing,
three days and three nights atop mine new home,
three days and three nights rising to tides beckon,
three days and three nights from that time I near drowned.
"Answer me this Lord! How much longer?
How much longer this vast sea to roam?"
Impatient praying with absolute conviction,
thirsty, tired, freezing and hungry, seemed like forever; lost and forlorn.

XXXII

Moments of clarity then dead driftwood slumber,
upon mackerel I feasted and spat out their bones,
no clump of land spied just epic seascape proportion,
held close mine commission; it remained my last hope.
We are created for company, for friendship and favour,
hearts beat for family and loves fond embrace,
I fear mine strength ebbed and fully then wavered,
to sleeps restless dungeon mine frail frame collapsed.

XXXIII

Thudded loud, mine world spun askew,
mine vessel bumped, cleaved by brute force in two,
I startled, dazed, alerted from still,
a shadow tall protruded through the grey mist.
A ship! Ahoy! Mine heart didst excite jump,
ropes flung down, around me tied.... then up,
lowered onto deck mine hawser loosed,
observed by a crew clutched dispassionately in groups.

XXXIV

This a flotilla of no vagabond command,
naval force of four I counted, merchant grand,
formation regimented, royal insignia at mast,
crew uniformed in cut cloth identifiable by rank.
Introduced they the Commander, a realms Earl no less,
Uxbury his name in gold braid epaulettes,
at his right hand a secretary, Uxbury's constant silhouette,
loyal companion's blade ready to counter all threats.

XXXV

"Explain yerself," Uxbury enquired in rich tones eloquent,
"Explain why thou be found these prevailing currents?
Malevolent the seas; ourselves battled through the storm.
How didst thou survive without subjected harm?"
I composed mine situation, pointed out mine defunct plank,
flung o'erboard by brigands, the sea I near drowned drank,
told Uxbury I a preacher of The Lord's Holy Word,
asked a pointed question - if the gospel he had heard?

XXXVI

Drawing deep breath Uxbury gripped tight the guard rail,
grew a deathly pallor, his blood from face pale drained,
then from low intestine a moan found groans release,
stared me down, his neck lined in angers bulging crease.
"Thou art a blatherskite, a gas bag, a raving lunatic,
a ranter, an incandescent manipulator of the weak.
I charge thee here now with words that thou hast already heard,
I believe the time has come once again to churn thee o'erboard."

XXXVII

Suddenly a miracle The Lord's faithfulness didst provide,
Hark! A bellow from watchman, crow's nest high.
He pointed to the water abreast starboard side
and with fierce deliberation Uxbury side stepped to the right.
Mish-mash and debris floated upon the waves,
half a length of keel, helm, flag and torn sail;
my former ship had succumbed to recent storms impale.
"Look! Sire!" I roared eagerly, "Without me they failed!"

XXXVIII

There were no survivors visible from midst of deck,
all souls violently despatched to seas dark depth black,
I thought of the faces, of the preaching pleading frank,
all now in satan's grip except perhaps he who cast mine plank.
I pointed, spoke to Uxbury, saw fright alight his eyes,
"The Lord has placed me safely here, mine ejection He repaid,
He will administer youse the same cursed fate
if youse premeditatedly propel me to waters murky grave!!"

XXXIX

The Earl staggered, his breath he didst slow rasp,
shoulders stooped, his hands to head he clasped,
took a minute his countenance fought compose,
then exercising caution from seat he slow arose.
"Yer heart be full of bluster," I confronted; then asked him why?
"I perceive Earl of Uxbury, youse art fraid to die!"
In voice quiet he beckoned secretary his trembling aside,
instructed me to ships hold; mine death now twice denied.

XL

"Bozeman Edwards," he introduced self, held hand out for exchange,
"We shall call thee Jonah! Like he from scripture's page,
Uxbury ist a fair man but you've rattled his stalwart cage,
we've nare seen him flummoxed, such fear nare fore displayed.
I've seen him in heat of battle, at ease in royal of court,
served him best of twenty summers, I now forty from mine birth.
We sail for King Henry, nay know if this you've heard....."

Thought I...his mission from a man but knew mine was of The Lord.

Part Two

Beyond the Consequence of Fear...

It is the folly of kings to plot and plan;
to endorse the industry of ruthless men.

BEYOND THE CONSEQUENCE OF FEAR

I

For two days I slept mine body comatose cold,
that restful deep sleep where nare a sound is heard,
awoke I eventually, confused... I wondered where,
remembered then the navy ship and mine rescue from despair.
New fresh cloth linens they had left upon a chair,
some warm crusts, an apple, flagons elixir fair,
I dressed and gorged the vitals, tried compose mine windswept hair
and urging shaken confidence stepped out to sea salts air.

II

Life aboard appeared busy, men dutied to their chores,
some nodded politely while some chose to me ignore,
here a greet familiar, there a nonchalant stare,
Jonah some addressed me; mine memory now full clear.
Men laboured at deck cleansing, some portside mending sails,
others toiled at large ropes scraping weed and shells,
some sat sword sharpening humming sailors verse,
Officers specifying orders while those hardened mumbled curse.

III

Mine limbs were boldly aching, mine strength I vowed restore,
I spent the morning walking, stretching out the tired,
if asked to assist with any task I made mine time to stop
and laboured with all vigour expending energy's last drop.
Underneath to galley the cook he bid mine step
to wash buckets of potatoes and deflower them of their skins,
we served one hundred sailors their nourishment and brew
I then commanded to Quarters to bring Earl Uxbury his food.

IV

The Earl was conducting a meeting, ubiquitous Edwards at his side,
Officers sequestered from all four ships that early spring eve-tide,
half a dozen charts spread, lit by lantern bright,
lands and isles identifiable with our voyage position tracked.
Uxbury bid me serve his troop of hungry men,
Bozeman instructed each plates release conveyed with nod or grin,
stood I at the Quarters rear where I observed each eating bunch;
keeping mine words to mere courtesies but listening twice as much.

V

By insignia he an Admiral, an Earl of titled rank,
cousin to King Henry; to rule the seas his Right.
Shoulders full to hair thick, framed to six feet tall,
aged to bout five decades with wrinkles lined and drawn.
A natural leader Uxbury, worked he his crew with ease,
considered all opinions even those comments that displeased,
a father figure to his men, he held in high regard,
responsibility taken for all decisions; those simple and those hard.

VI

The measure of a man be taken when oft tempers flare,
Uxbury a wise counsel kept the climate fair,
any sign of dissention the Earl would ask for facts,
dates and records requested with language weaved with tact.
Uxbury a husband to a stately comely wife,
two sons assigned to royal court, a younger not yet despatched
and Bozeman Edwards his emissary and his confidant,
two working, trusting; without fear or daunt.

VII

Edwards constituted a clever man, a man of verse and rhyme,
educated to letters, disposition born to smile,
no one knew his pedigree, a secret so well kept,
assigned to work with Uxbury some twenty summers past.
They communicated with signs that only each they knew,
a gesture by face or hand accompanied with words so few.
Bozeman the Earls right arm, their relationship close-knit,
it said that if Uxbury drew his sword, Edwards would be holding it!

VIII

So it was 'pon that ship I laboured into night,
they wrestling o'er tidal charts till near the morning bright,
decisions made and ratified, Uxbury seemed well pleased,
stood he then when all at end to instruct the crew's release.
Trooped they out upon the deck down ropes flung from conceal,
the ragged bunch limbered down to oars-boat waiting three
and harkened each to their sleeps nest
adrift the pale light sea.

IX

A blank stare from Uxbury, he drawn tired it seemed,
a smile of gratitude from Edwards I received,
each their separate direction took to climb their berths to sleep,
I charged to clean the Quarters afore I took mine leave.
Eventually tasks completed, I yawned, mine eyes red blurred,
head hit pillowed cushion contemplating some detail I had heard,
if true this wouldst be an adventure like none I'd been 'pon,
then drifted I to drowsy rest; mine strength ebbed, all but gone.

X

Squeak rude honk of sea gull squall stirred mine resting shape,
visible from port side hole a clamour birds deranged,
for from atop the cook didst drop bloodied chum beyond the rails
and baying birds swooped quickly down to gorge beaks taste remains.
Flutter storm, one thousand wings attacked with frenzied zeal,
haphazard flight o'er head fore scraping clean the waves.
Watched I while pondering what this day I could achieve,
noticed I the Commander and Edwards beckon I perceived.

XI

Bozeman took the tiller, the conversation to steer,
looked out across the vastness, coughed; his voice to clear,
"The Earl is of substance, a man of abundant wealth,
believes King Henry is acquiring the Uxbury legacy by stealth.
Estate and villages north London, in city a bankers square,
when ordered on one year's commission his conscience roared – beware!"
Somehow they me trusted and wished this here divulge,
I kept mine tongue tight; their lips further to indulge.

XII

"The Uxbury heritage was hard fought; established o'er time,"
the Earl expanded, "It will pass to mine son 'pon mine dying.
Henry is mine cousin, he older me by five,
son of Conqueror William who shaped young Henry's mind.
While we are family he I treat with fearful respect,
ever reverent; I exceedingly vigilant.
For you see Henry has designs, an empire he to build,
an army to ready fore bloods crimson tide be spilled."

XIII

They shifted uncomfortably, a sign for mine now speak,
Uxbury surveyed his charges while Edwards bit his lip,
time seemed to pause; sands slowed their shuffling drop,
waited I to witness if reveal had anchored stop.
"Jonah: the Earl fears you for you are known by God,
it would appear that no deceit resides 'pon thine heart,
nothing, he feels, you leave from unblemished mouth unsaid,
with manner brusque he has suggested you'd antagonise the dead!"

XIV

I considered the intriguing duo; mine visage gave a twitch,
I irked internally yet displayed no displeasure 'pon mine face,
"A compliment I'm sure, though yer words wouldst make some weep,
I appreciate yer candour and the trust of subsequent reap.
I shall take yer disclosures and ask Almighty God,
by prayer I'll petition the True and Sovereign Lord,
a few thoughts quick strike me; I'll tarry nay mine words,
accommodate me gentlemen while mine assault o truth be heard."

XV

"Yer tale suggests King Henry ist a canny wily man,
yet it is not a cousin he craves but loyalty his demand,
his person be driven by wealth and powers blind leaning,
dignity o character lies far from this fellows scheming.
Be careful Earl that it is not yer wife that he doth plot,
like David who Bathsheba spied bathing from his roof,
for you Earl could be King Henry's very own Uriah,
finding yerself force exiled sailing forth toward yer doom!"

XVI

Apoplectic fury overtook the measured one,
the Earl charged with one intent to cast me o'erboard,
Bozeman cut in, shielding us from fist fight
for I was poised ready to punch the olde Earl down.
Then pausing... Uxbury put his mitts down,
took a step back, laughing now from frown.
They knew now I'd forcibly give mine own back,
that I not fraid of earthly titles and nay fraid to drown.

XVII

I left the gents at helm to journey across mine day,
cast a wary eye out, mine odds continued weigh,
half expected a malicious mob to instigate murders slay
or perhaps they'd wait for darkened hour to slice me on mine way.
But the hours travelled quietly, I set mine hands to chore,
I laboured, cut and crafted then polished smooth an oar,
tended table for the cook fore disappearing down mine berth,
prayed that night by candlelight for a poor world drenched in hurt.

XVIII

Sabbath morn was born; faint sun broke through the stars,
with me a few gathered; the outcasts and the scarred,
ten men my companions to praise The Mighty Lord,
ten men listening intently the sharing of His Word.
A tentative step took Uxbury, he shifted behind a mast,
seemed he to listen to the words of God's salvation grace,
wondered I his intentions for his motivations he well hid:
was he searching for a blessing or some shill to do his bid?

XIX

So it was when at our end the Earl made his approach,
held in check his last few steps lest our huddle he encroach,
I took mine leave The Lord's marked ten and Uxbury I joined,
watching together the calm blue sea out came the words he coined.
"Jonah, thou art an honest man... insightful... truthful to a fault,
hold thee no prejudice, no proclivity toward idol god,
Edwards suggests you meet with us, our mission to reveal,
we'd appreciate an accommodation; the favour of God's seal."

XX

"He canst be bought with words soft coughed," I started to reply
Uxbury interjected declaring an immediate deny.
"Desireth we His blessing, His hand upon this ship,
for we venture forth to Rome but that nay end this trip,
Jerusalem our beckon; the apple of His eye,
thus we'll plough these heavy seas and I fearful lest we die.
Jonah, I now accept that thou art answerable to The Lord,
however I be responsible to Henry... ships four and all aboard."

XXI

Jerusalem, Jerusalem, mine heart near cleaved in two,
celestial of all cities; the place of His own choose,
the buttress mine imagination; mine longing from afar,
the pivot place of history where Christ spent His own last hours.
Jerusalem, Jerusalem, mine feet they staggered stepped,
I clasped hold of Uxbury and nodded mine consent,
nare fore in life excitement such like built
and from mine heart I thanked The Lord for rescue 'pon this ship.

XXII

For the retention of excitement ebbs when life becomes a trial,
when ambitions breath is ravaged like the pressing of a vine,
seasons of favour blessing then circumstances contrive,
each day descending slowly while one clings to mortal life.
But within such wrestle comes reveal, the reveal of nugget bright,
a field abundant plenty, a hidden pearl of prize,
such it has been these decade years, mine past life much forgot,
destination now Jerusalem, awakening a prophecy from The Lord.

XXIII

While in prayer some years past I discerned His soft of voice,
"Jerusalem! Jerusalem!" mine heart I heard it twice,
no matter how dark, His promise I didst not spurn;
to preach in His city and at all time end to witness His return.
Today I am revived, mine heart within sings,
abundant joy a plenty after feasting lean on crumbs,
waited I impatiently marking down each slow sprung hour,
ventured then to Quarters and pounded full the door.

XXIV

Entry to dim candle-shine, a desk arranged with chairs,
Edwards with a key chest hung extracted parchment from a drawer
and seeming somewhat hesitant echo paced the wood sprung floor.
"To stimulate some context mine words I shall not enhance,
for you see Jonah, Henry is a disruptor of all royal circumstance,
initially hated by his brothers was confined to Normandy home,
allied with William junior after whom Henry seized the throne:
he subsequently defeated Robert, incarcerating him behind stone."

XXV

"King Henry," continued Bozeman, "He seems to thrive on threats,
yea power doth nay suit a poor man
and Henry's realm is pecuniarily stretched.
His desire is to muster an army, for foes to bludgeon stop,
to dissuade any foreigner's actions and their invasion attempts usurp.
England be an island and the seas he desires to rule,
so he aims to strike mammon's alliance
whilst selling royal dispensation's bargain as his tool."

XXVI

"Most rulers stoop to tithes tax rob and purse pinch infiltration,
sufficient grab their mammon nab keeping swathes in degradation,
concentrate they their powers on constructing laws
against mutinous insurrection.
Henry thinks beyond the norm, his mind a Catherine Wheel,
his ambitions roar by plot and sword still remain unfilled,
hence our voyage to Rome's own Pope, Henry's aspirations to convene
for England's shores are scythed to death with little left to glean."

XXVII

"The more I hear o yer fine king, the more I fear he fraud,
feasting full off Lazarus' back; licking clean his sores,
the rich man died to Hades scream to sit in fire and flame;
that rich man lives again today and Henry ist his name!"
Mine anger wrought a terse deep tone, mine innards blood enflamed,
mine stomach's bile began to boil I continued have mine say,
"The rich young ruler hast grown olde, by covets reach still snared,
imagine Henry and the Pope; an unlikely match well paired!"

XXVIII

"Enough," roared the Earl, "If it please thee let us have our say,
plenty time to involve thee later these details to debate.
Henry desires Rome's backing, the Pope's crusader army to engage,
our travel then to Jerusalem to harvest olden routes of trade,
like Nebuchadnezzar, Pharaoh... Alexander of history page
Henry sees himself a King like those of ancient days."
I looked and smiled at Uxbury and swallowed down mine dread,
"They'll soon have one thing in common; for soon they'll be all dead!"

XXIX

"Canst thou keep thine lips tight shut?
Hast thou not learnt from Bible's James?
Control thine tongue, retain thine thoughts,
mine poor heart please assuage.
King Henry aspires to Eden's gold,
Mesopotamia's wealth and means,
to transport its loads via olde Rome's roads,
to pave his empire dreams."

XXX

Apologised I shame faced red, signalled mine comply,
suggested I had reason suspended urging excitement in its way!
Not wishing the Earl mine further scold in quieted voice meek spoke,
"So it seems Earl, if it please; Henry for gold doth lust!"
"Not just that," came curt reply, "but commercial silver too,
facilitating him his full sought right all coinage to control,
a new idea he possesses; o'er time he smart deduced,
rebase to debase all currency with parchment receipts introduce."

XXXI

"He who holds the gold can direct and with-hold spending,
canst through the realm a stately nation guide,
pull the strings one way and defraud by price inflation
else usury rates decrease to increase funds taxation.
A parchment receipt is an instrument, mere token for the bearer,
but at construction the King can play disguise;
if one can control manufacturer's inks, well every now and then,
one couldst stamp official parchment beyond the power of ten!"

XXXII

"The poor are always indigent; it is the wealthy Henry's after,
by fear of threat he'll bend them to his will,
so yes he requires gold but there is a lot more silver
and his parchment backed by this ore will purchase many men.
First stop Rome, the Pope's army to inveigle,
we'll solicit the city's bishop under royal authority,
obsequious will be our bow, facilitating terms bonded legal
then sail for Jerusalem under the duo's sovereign decree."

XXXIII

The Earl stood back smiling as if it fate accomplished,
I looked, he nodded his consent mine speak he gave.
"Regarding the Pope, I believe with yellow he enamoured;
with gold that glints he'll sure desire his share."
"Quite right Jonah," Edwards added, "men have on each their measure,
for both Titles have convened together afore.
We'll utilise gold's sparring for our trading barter,
to appear hard fought the terms our charter's royal engage."

XXXIV

"Two devils," I exclaimed, "Rogues! Duplicitous deceivers,
instead o wood; crosses o fool's gold they'll bear.
Methinks each man doth believe that he is Caesar
and calamitous design will find them both residing in satan's lair!"
Bozeman smiled, turned toward his master,
Uxbury non-committal refused engage his stare,
"Sire Opulent!" muttered Bozeman. "The Pope be called by Henry!"
"Lo! Keep thine words to self Bozeman; thou drive us to despair!"

XXXV

Uxbury stood, paced to shelved decanter,
paused... drew cup long against the vine.
Stopped. Looked for reason to continue,
shifting slowly locked his eyes with mine.
"Fifty, fifty our offer on golden bullion,
Pope be pleased; we'll keep silver set aside,
he'll release to me authority o'er his Crusade army,
deposits paid we'll wrest the seas east tide."

XXXVI

"Jonah, there ist one word whose power thou canst deny,
each time it spoke, alert it glint thine eyes,
Jerusalem, The Lord's own city doth render thee speechless,
I'll herald its name forever for thine speech wouldst quick run dry!
Honorius' Crusader ten by thousands will strengthen our endeavour,
shall keep the Kings of east their hunger bayed,
willst strike the fear of death 'pon foe's bearing
and journey us back to England fore the stretch of next year's day."

XXXVII

Quarters silent, the seamless duo reposed 'pon repast,
drained slow their mead as if objective's relay past,
I sat, feigned off proffered sustenance content,
mine thoughts to collect; considerations to digest.
"Babylon meets baal," I ventured. "Which city I canst decide worse,
London and Rome; both factions it wouldst appear have Christ lost.
Gents I fear that this is a quest compassed 'pon disaster,
betwixt the stealth, no good I'm sure willst come."

XXXVIII

The Earl choked, Edwards immediated to his master,
Uxbury caught his breath, let his anger's wrath subside.
"It is our instruction lest we suffer execution's warrant,
what thou prefer Jonah: each us innocent to die?"
Bozeman discombobulated rose and at me pointed,
"Beyond fear this journey we commanded,
the King's ambition; for his cerebral empire holds he dear,
baptised Henry our journey; one that goes beyond the consequence of fear."

XXXIX

"The ambition of greedy men is always ill conceived,
for mammon's barn willst fast to o'erflow
leaving more space required by avarice's eyes to hold."
I said mine words, bid mine night; arose mine steps to leave.
Earl Uxbury stood mine hand to shake and clutched mine linen sleeve.
"Jonah, thou art blessed with bravery, free speech enjoyed by few,
I ask please assist Bozeman, act for us a sounding board,
render us thine measured thoughts... any words o'er heard."

XL

I stood outside, surveyed the heavy brooding,
purple calloused clouds bruise punched the sky,
the ship beat the waves pushing us forward,
four crews oblivious; their mission cleverly disguised.
Gold and politics make poor companions,
mixed together they become concoctions deadly brew,
tomorrow or next day we'll draw secure to quayside,
considered mine leave for the perilous things I knew.

Part Three

Skulk ye Devils the Darkened Halls…

*Trod we first, pace gentle,
then plough we each our own Akel Dama,
all in search for gold's bloody prize.*

SKULK YE DEVILS THE DARKENED HALLS

I

Awoke to last March day to sound of pattered raining,
I charged with preparation chores by day then spent,
reflected 'pon Henry's quote beyond the consequence of fear,
me thoughts a better statement – an odyssey beyond sense!
The crew discerned that hatchers plan was brooding
for the Earl's mood stiffened rigid by the hour,
it be same any ship soon close of mission,
be found busy lest one succumbs to commands ill-tempered fire!

II

I ordered to the Earl's Quarters later hour that evening,
he to decide what numbers canter his aside,
too large a force wary be Rome's citizenry,
too small a bunch displayed; at he they'd only laugh.
Flags agreed, provisions then debated,
less time there spent, he figured two days most,
Uxbury happier on seas for he despised politics gamble,
distrusted he foreign swords blacksmithed to cut and thrust.

III

April first; perhaps we the fools to death's grim dicing,
Porto di Traiono at Civitavecchia's coastline,
Trajan's port for nearer Rome was silted,
plenty room, four ships to berth portside.
The quayside noised of industry, swelled with labour's busy,
toughened men, vigorous, sweat lined,
experted in art of ropes and lifting netted tonnage,
stevedores hastened readied at each our ships aside.

IV

Bozeman expelled the hardened grumbling litter,
the paws of port authority he expected to grease line.
A royal commission tendered Edwards in explanation,
bribes paid for mercenary guard to pretend ships safely supervised.
Bozeman comprehended port life and their ways of working,
monies required to quench surprise of fire,
it unwritten that if a paid hull succumbed to thieveries temptation,
perpetrators wouldst be killed stone dead by cruel axed expire.

V

Instructed he I to visit each ship's skipper,
orders circulated that short wouldst be our stay,
crews surprised for their leave they had been waiting,
cavilled grievances for taverns wouldst not secure their wage!
The belly of the fourth hull I deftly descended,
stabled horses ordered prepared for expedition's fray,
handsome beasts of purebred muscled sinew
were saddled tall with coats of arms displayed.

VI

Our retinue determined, focused 'pon adventure,
Magi force mounted lined in train,
ten armed emblazoned flag-bear fighters at the front,
ten red stationed rear with sharpened blades.
Accompanied by Captains two an apprenticed cook looked nervous,
a provisions guard positioned with mixed roped crates,
wild nostril flare tore up Civitavecchia's cobbles,
set to Capital's destination some forty miles away.

VII

Hard ride day punctuated by mile-stones granite,
we journeyed through farmlands of peasants bent at toil,
they stopped to witness our steed's paced momentum,
bare frugal living those scavengers of soil.
I prayed as we rode for Christ died for these people,
we passed them again by forest and crop pastures green field fold,
same the world over, it populated by misery,
a special blessing, His great love for the poor.

VIII

In the wake of two score, seven hills approacheth,
we adjourned, built a coal-side for smokes rise dine,
o'er mists hills groaned Rome's thoroughfare precincts,
faint charms of bell toll harbingered night.
Uxbury set a guard positioned at angles,
concerned lest some outlaws pillage and leave us to remains,
Bozeman requested me toward some tale telling,
considered I options fore mine tongue loosed memories chains.

IX

"Rome," I started, "desires Babylonian status,
Nebuchadnezzar's head gold now the Pope's ambitious hold,
septenary hill tops composed by past Emperors,
each paving their paths; their legacies unfold.
Upkeep by slaves, stones perishing columns,
requiring facades repairing by vast sums o ore,
armies past legions to garrisons far reaching,
legends o brave soldiers; the valiant and bold."

X

Those sitting by fire side warmed to vines story,
even the Earl smirked the words I chose,
continued the city's history by tall tale,
cadenced the timing, striking the blows.
"I'll tell youse o Caesar, Julius Emperor,
a military genius his conquest of Gaul,
rebuilt he Carthage and Grecian's fine Corinth
but his end was brutal, by knife plunge his unfold."

XI

"Blood be the currency acquired by all rulers,
power o'er life to exact tightened hold,
Augustus took the reins, Tiberius, Caligula,
Claudius to Nero who fiddle crazed his bow.
A monster that heathen, burnt he the city,
by full cocked madness he extinguished his foes,
gladiatorial rampage and Roman candle carnage,
blood o the martyrs; the killing o Paul."

XII

"Exported they havoc's violent disorder,
Vespasian's son Titus undertook Jerusalem's sack,
not one stone left unturned as prophesised by Jesus,
supplemented Titus his campaign by cruel hunger attack."
"We'll leave it for now," interrupted Earl Uxbury,
"We need rest our frames to keep the morrow's brain wise.
I thank thee Jonah for passing these dark hours,
Edwards change the guard and gents... watch thine backs."

XIII

Weary at rise for sleep was 'pon damp furze,
broke fast then marshalled equines cavalcade,
Uxbury us circled to convey mandates mission,
position made clear fore we each charged the reins.
"We canst straight sojourn to the Pope's pearly palace,
there is procedure to follow lest he us attack.
King Henry advised passage to the College of Cardinals;
call to the Chancellor who sits on Pope's right."

XIV

Bore we our trail through broad roads stone cobbled,
passing facades glory to man's temporal reign,
Pantheon's granite and spherical rooftop,
baal's administration where all idol gods are praised.
Forum's colonnades, illustrious boulevard,
stretched o'er bones of catacombed graves,
past Colosseum's hideous courtyard,
scene which bathed citizens in believer's death screams.

XV

Shook me to bones, hair pin prick tingle,
trots gallop through drawbridge to opulent reside,
Deaconry Maria Nuova home of papal advisor,
Aymeric de la Chatre; Chancellor the Wise.
Our troop armed to guard line the Earl he dismounted,
manservant of the Cardinal a purpose enquired,
King's sealed authority handed, waxed red embossed,
the servant to hallway inside disappeared.

XVI

Past a short sand drop the door bolt didst open,
a long gangly fellow in red robes wore with pride,
Uxbury bowed with gracious endeavour,
the Cardinal though didst our entry deny.
"We charged by King Henry, Pope Honorius to call on,
a legal bind fellowship he wishes him sign."
"Fraid thats impossible," hesitated the Cardinal,
"For six weeks past dearest Honorius didst die!"

XVII

"Dead!" echoed Edwards, the Earl just stood speechless,
"Dead!" repeated Bozeman, "our journey in vain!
Eight weeks we've sailed through winter fierce waters,
ship of four battered by leviathan's harsh waves.
This mission of madness to avoid Henry's warrant,
deposed at our end by Honorius' fresh grave!"
"Silence," instructed Uxbury, the Cardinal too pondered,
he then bid us entry his grand roman estate.

XVIII

Three we entered through marbles sculpted hallway,
windows of tall bathed home in light,
ornaments, furnishings of sumptuous comfort,
palatial surroundings in contrast poor's plight.
Uxbury and Edwards accustomed to prosperity,
I too from mine past but long days since seen,
entered an office of capacious proportion,
bid he us welcome with extend of his ring.

XIX

In all things inhabits society's structured order,
but The Lord Himself said – the last will be first,
Uxbury considered the Cardinal's proffered finger
then a nod to me signalled the Commander's confront.
I stood forward bewildered and role played anger,
stared down Rome's agent, he expectant mine lip,
turned mine two fellows, Bozeman's face straining,
trying real hard to hold in his laugh.

XX

"Sire. Have ye heard the words o our loving Saviour?
Call no one father this earthly domain!
For there is One, He Majesty, Royal King o Heaven,
it is He whom I serve not Rome's power grab knave!
You serve a Pope, these two King Henry
but ye no different in God's eyes to any other men.
I dare not kiss idol gold's folding,
mine loyalty to another I'll surely not feign."

XXI

Aymeric gurned, his face leaned to crease fold,
ready to unleash... but of emotion took hold,
dismissed me from his side turned to the Earl
though visibly smarting for mine words had hit home.
"Ah! A believer," he smile practiced at Uxbury,
"these days, if I honest, there are so few in Rome,
mostly devils skulking these corridors of wrestling,
all seeking favour plus those plotting for throne."

XXII

I watched the Cardinal, his eyes quenched to narrow,
covets glare revealed, locked in crowed lines,
"So, my liege, I gather eight weeks sailing,
the news then of Honorius' death by time you denied.
Tell me gentlemen the reason of calling,
perhaps 'pon the matter I can shed some light!"
He bid the Earl sit, behind stationed Edwards,
I pointed to doorway and there took mine stand.

XXIII

"Explain to me first," queried Earl Uxbury,
"What has occurred since Honorius' death?
I believe if Canon is administered correctly,
an election is held, a new Pope to be blessed."
"Indeed, you correct sire, that held the next morning,
our votes we collected to sanction the spoil,
when I had counted elections fold paper,
found not one Pope elected... instead we have two!"

XXIV

"Devils indeed," I added with bluster,
the Earl me admonished, I diverted mine eyes,
then looking at Aymeric, the Earl gently encouraged,
"explain us further fore I relinquish our prize!"
Hands to face, triangled with fingers,
the Cardinal drew breath, his thoughts to compose,
"Romulus and Remus, this city of two founders,
now Frangipani and Pierleoni – two families at feud!"

XXV

Piqued our attention, we settled lesson history,
strange bed-fellows plot the Cardinal's expose,
two wealthy families each fronting a candidate,
both nominations vying for power.
Gregorio Papareschi for team Frangipani
had sixteen senior Cardinals and most Europe's kings,
Pietro Pierleoni of same named family,
twenty four younger College members voted for him.

XXVI

"Pietro now Anacletus had more vote numbers
yet Gregorio was offered the office, his backing unique,
he took the name Innocent, the second that title,
to him I gave loyalty, for me he is Rome's Prince.
So we now have two Popes with added confusion,
one soon may draft hemlock and wither away,
so tell me gracious Earl, reveal to me thine mission,
lest I extend mine rejection and set thee on way."

XXVII

By acts subtle subterfuge Uxbury baffled the Cardinal,
unsealed the embossed, Henry's fine parchment scroll,
lied that Henry looking to finance defences,
the strengthening of England: fiefdom loyal to the Pope.
Wouldst take backing of Crusade, Pope's foreign army,
six months at most, control of the tolls,
trade route pillage, commission's extraction,
for Innocent's backing both realms wouldst split gold.

XXVIII

The Cardinal's eyes glistened like nuggets fine lust dusting,
"A daring plan from Henry... well conceived!
If there is money in it I will introduce you to Innocent,
he is seeking a bounty for... churches to build!
Earl if it pleases we'll draw up documents,
a legal necessity, a requirement if thou please?"
"Agreed," fashioned the Earl as he beckoned to Edwards,
"We've readied them forehand; if terms you have agreed."

XXIX

We sat that eve-tide by fire coals red banter,
reflecting the day; the morrow meet Pope.
Bozeman insightful ventured Aymeric's loyalty to Innocent,
but if we to secure treasure, we ought meet Popes both!
Uxbury agreed for he had discerned that measure,
"fear not Bozeman for I've devised mine own plan,
nought tell Aymeric for he blinded by covets craving,
to Anacletus already I've despatched mine own man!"

XXX

Stead a cross, atop his head he wore a lofty crown,
sculpted daintily with gemstone emeralds raw.
A soldier's face; as comfortable in a palace as a trench,
Innocent: far from suffering this Isaiah's servant.
"Heard thou not bow, nor kiss thine sovereign's ring,"
to me his distain with curse of words assailed,
"Careful Pope lest youse be by whale swallowed!"
I laughed... "Or better yet be struck by lightnings engage."

XXXI

Uxbury gasped, rushed Innocent's distressed aside,
clasped his hand and commanded me outside,
"Temple pillagers," I roared with diction growing bolder,
"In the place o mercy ye two Pharisees chose gold!"
Bozeman informed later 'pon their deed,
a split in ore, the Pope's army too released,
fixed positions across the Holy Land of olde,
six months they'd threat violence; King Henry's ships to load.

XXXII

The Earl promised a penalty for the barbs I had let slip,
"later Jonah," he remarked for he invested in conniver's grip,
held he letters of Pope's affirming, clasped them tight to chest,
Aymeric waited patiently to swindle his handler's snip.
"Earl Uxbury if it please thee, a percentage due is fair,
for I to Innocent introduced thee; brought to Papal lair."
A bag of coin was offered, it disappeared by hand of sleight,
Aymeric too under instruction; accompany us through the night.

XXXIII

Not so innocent Frangipani's man, he wily's clever fox,
set the Chancellor to ride to port to enclose us in his box,
ensure no meet with Anacletus; keep Uxbury from Pierleoni's gates,
Innocent protecting his investment for his enemy he didst hate.
We stopped and built a campsite,
Bozeman plied the Pope's emissaries with wine.
Out from cover darkness our provisioner to the Earl inclined,
the two then disappearing to the sound of hoof thump whine.

XXXIV

If Innocent be clever well then twice so the Earl,
for the provisioner wast Captain Dare of Henry's ship third,
I had recognised his swagger, at his wink I bit mine lip,
Aymeric and guards flat out, by shrewdness given slip.
So off they rode to Anacletus,
for him the extend of bribe,
to return with letters later,
Innocent's sharp-wittedness by alcohol denied.

XXXV

Comforts sleep was kicked awake by boot of leathered force,
mine eyes blinked to consciousness, mine ears to coarse assault,
"Fool!" enraged the Chancellor, "Where ist Uxbury gone?"
"I've searched each corner the encampment, by subterfuge his run!"
"Cardinal," I beckoned, "Sit by mine aside,
explain to me what ails youse for by sleep I occupied."
Aymeric drew long breath explained his tale of woe,
mine brain working o'er time, mine desire his fury slow."

XXXVI

Later I examined if I complicit in illicits wrongful gain,
was I party to deception as the Earl played dangers game
for the Cardinal I subdued, then subjected him to blame,
charged him with embezzlement for seeking purse's claim.
Told the tale of Gehazi, Elisha's trusted aid
who cheated Naaman the Syrian; for a miracle requested pay,
"for youse Cardinal are trusted by God the poor's souls to care,
repent or disobedients punishment youse willst soon justly bear."

XXXVII

Through the foliage walked Uxbury dressed in his night wear,
Aymeric charged him with treason, the Earl quick feigned non care,
listened intently to the Cardinal then offered rehearsed solution,
something raw had been eaten; he forced to severe ablution.
Steely eyed the Cardinal his face gathered its compose,
tendered the Earl his apologies and to his tent arose.
To me Uxbury extended gratitude, his handshake cleared our air,
yet truth I had garnished to Aymeric; mine conscience fully cleared.

XXXVIII

Our third morning spring fine, we rose to merriment cheer,
Uxbury signalled success to Bozeman who whispered news mine ear,
to Civitavecchia we departed, relaxed at comforts pace,
our expectation soon departure for East's mysterious embrace.
We lunched somewhere bout noontime, the Cardinal still in train,
he sat by the Earl thrashing out their final plot details,
instructions for the army the Cardinal conveyed,
their final handshake confirming how Rome's gold be paid.

XXXIX

With bout an hour to ride I reflected 'pon our path,
Rome a sticky cauldron, soaked in power and stealth.
Europe's kings fraid of Innocent, they believe he holds heaven's key
and they'll perpetrate all crime of fraud to keep the charlatan pleased.
Three Popes, one dead, now two on separate thrones,
both in the pocket of Henry swayed by covets hold.
If plot discovered to Henry's cost and he finds his spirit banished,
I suppose he can go to Rome's Pope to pay handsomely his penance!

XL

Aymeric took leave at ship by port off Civitavecchia's quay,
the Earl suggested he we follow to Quarters for debrief,
at gangplank stood a fellow, Henry's enseige his standard revealed,
handed a scroll to the Commander which he feverishly unsealed.
With an almighty bellow the parchment fell to floor,
Uxbury his chest grasped we he assisted to a chair.
King Henry as suspected had changed the course his life,
had taken possession of Uxbury's estates and imprisoned his fair wife.

Part Four

Plough the Horizon...

Regression is the enemy of adventure.
Plough the horizon toward fruitful bounty.

PLOUGH THE HORIZON

I

Leadership oft doth bear the brunt, for life doth toll extract,
some born to administrative privilege, by experience others contract,
a leader takes responsibility for chore or quests engage,
directing minutia of efforts whilst measuring successes gauge.
Respect doth not automatically follow the person in control
for worker bees oft wallow in selfish moan and groan,
self seek the currency of the ego not prone to care,
one canst tell the type of leader by the spoils they choose to share.

II

Uxbury was the kind of man that emboldened each met fellow,
excellent with sword, no talent short with shot of quiver arrow,
he'd enflame each heart with words impart, of each mission showed no fear,
bore royal title's birthright yet of he his troops held dear.
Not normally swayed by emotion, the Earl was refine poised,
a fair adjudicator the machinations of men's minds,
had earned mine respect and favour though he'd nay ever be a friend,
the kind of man I'd follow toward any campaigns end.

III

Immediate to Quarters Earl Uxbury retired,
door bolted from inside we anticipated roars,
but silence rose intolerable,
apprehension didst abound.
Bozeman Edwards took the ship,
set departures flag unfurled,
the crew steadied to his orders,
each ship compassed to the south.

IV

I laboured deep that dark night, sleep I fraid took flight,
concerned I for Uxbury, prayed for his trial plight,
brought the urgency his wife, her plead afore Christ's throne
for Henry's stance deliberate to ensure the Earl came home.
Arose I to walks pace, encouraged early hour works crew,
discerned each the seriousness the little facts they knew,
then joined I sleepless Bozeman, with command he not least fazed,
sat together talking, our steps we tracked back traced.

V

"The Earl wouldst not appreciate our wilful trip neglect
and I trained in the art of sailing, to plough the horizon this ship,
sufficient for the Earl to rest, to regain his bright compose,
forthright willst be his demeanour when he doth soon emerge.
Success has been our granting, fair tact he plied in Rome,
securing negotiations first Aymeric then the signatory two Popes,
but Henry is sagacious, seeks his counsel from few wise,
London's deliberation now communicated, he'll assume the Earl advised."

VI

Impressed I was of Bozeman, his considerations deeply thought,
understood I then his importance, his service to his Earl,
twenty years trusting, experiences varied wide,
an honourable confidante Uxbury had employed to his aside.
"So Bozeman, three letters holds the Earl to combat any threat,
one from Henry, two from Rome, but he's trapped in the King's net,
I wonder who he will follow, The Lord or words o man,
or some scheme his own devising; the earth's three gods to out plan!"

VII

"You're not here long Jonah but of matters you've made handle,
God's Holy Spirit seems to you well guide.
Answer me this Jonah, a question seemingly laughable;
of the two Popes which do you believe wears infallibles disguise?"
Laughter's release was palpable; events stress by mirth released,
"Smoke and mirrors Bozeman for only by Blood God's wrath be pleased,
not by mans idolatry, vain plotting or delusion,
especially works o three men to whose lives time willst bring conclusion."

VIII

"So Jonah, Christ Jesus paid the price,
by grace, free salvation through His Blood,
God's mercy, by His Son; His only Son begotten,
paid the penalty mine sins fully from mine birth?"
"Yes Bozeman, that ist the miracle o Calvary,
on a wooden cross Christ Jesus died by nail,
three days later His full life resurrected,
new life given freely for those who choose Him by faith."

IX

Bozeman scanned the morns horizon, his thoughts to contemplate,
I sat silent, mine eyes held fast the waves,
charting our course toward milk and honey's land of promise,
these same seas sailed by Paul in ancient days.
Brave men those early disciples, called He each to follow,
many finding their end by scorn to martyr's grave.
Bozeman turned to me; he smiled and simply nodded,
our moment passed, hands now pressed against helms gentle breeze.

X

Quarters tomb released the Earl the morrow's even-tide,
a glare of intensity didst 'pon his face reside,
detached he seemed, less tolerant as if the world despised,
to look at him a first response - the coldness of his eyes.
"Glad away from Rome?" I asked, short talked his aside,
"That infernal city no longer concerns for I seek a greater prize,
they allied with hob-goblins, with wizardries franchise;
your God Jonah willst deliver them His penalty's chastise."

XI

"Forty days our voyage to the city of your King,
mine King to service folly, for treasure to him bring,
Henry holds mine future, by his hands he gaoled mine wife,
thinkest I'll leave her to him to be killed by words her strife!
But lo she ist mine sweetheart, the mother of mine childs
the contempt I feel mine cousin doth poison mine insides,
to the power of ten Henry ranted, schemes like creeping weed..."
"More like," I interrupted, "print to the power of greed."

XII

Uxbury feigned a half heart, scorned twist of bile release,
clasped his fingers... balled... violence flowed to red veined wrists,
"I'll kill that madman, Jonah; mine vow I share with thee,
felt it in mine bones fore this expedition took her leave."
With rage of hate of words exchange, vulgar curse he didst explode,
stood there I silent and let his verbiage flow,
emotions cascade brittle, a sword upon his tongue,
slayed he all of London afore his temper done.

XIII

Sabbath drew our preaching group, we met our words to pray,
to signal Him our worship, to thank for each soul saved,
thirteen altogether, two additional since port,
I charged the Holy Word; their succour and their hope.
I chose mine words from Sermon's Mount,
Matthew's words I'd learnt verbait,
one ought forgive one's enemies;
exchange bitterness for grace.

XIV

"Twelve disciples Jonah, maybe a Judas in thine flock!"
for out stood the Earl of Uxbury, to listen and take stock,
"Jonah I watch thee preach, thine words cascade full flow,
telleth thou words of olde that each heart shouldst know,
convict thee many sinners, by times thou vexed mine mind,
I'll admit openly Jonah at times mine heart inclined.
However Jonah this fine day I fear I draw a line,
for Henry's act atrocious and God it seems turned blind."

XV

"How canst a King from Heaven, a Father to His child,
turn that babe to evil, mine soul to the unkind,
it senses not, not one jot, this fate I have succumbed
that God wouldst turn me over, instigate this dreadful harm!
Jonah thou preach angers frustration, bruise thou bended reeds,
thought it grace not legislation the gospel of thine plead,
the charge I prosecute afore thee, answer if thou please,
where art thine words of love; ist compassion in thine creed?"

XVI

"Upset mine Earl tis plain to see ye knowest not yer speak
for love is the very foundation, the words o mine critique,
these weeks there be little evidence that youse know The Lord,
no fruitful bounty forthcoming; no utterance Him yer heart,
nay the speak o salvation or The Lord's mercy grace,
ye crucify again the Son o Man, spit deceit about His face,
mine job to pull the heathen, to drag them out o hell,
for soon enough fair Earl for youse the tolling o His bell."

XVII

"Fore ye flip to yer defence answer me mine quest,
why do the heathen blame The Lord for humankind's digress?
The wicked wallow in self pity, youse no differ any man,
casting stones at He on High as if He answerable yer demands!
What Henry didst ist deplorable, ye guessed it fore this day,
suspected youse dishonesty fore departure 'pon the waves,
stead o blame be a man, consider whats be done,
steady yer plan but listen... wash insurrection from yer tongue!"

XVIII

"Jonah, sound thee kin mine father, he charged with mine chastise,
he to me it rarely given yet he always in the right,
to raise a child his responsibility, to grow mine frame to man,
dearly I'd love listen to his wisdom guide again.
Yet lo with thee I'm blessed now, a fair voice midst the beasts,
quick I wast to disparage, quick mine wrath's release,
mine apologies Jonah preacher, for words thee wisely spoke,
I'll take leave mine to Quarters and leave thee to thine work."

XIX

Watched I the Earl's slow step, shared I knowledge his pain,
yet futility's tongue wouldst credit him no profiteers gain,
turned again to Sabbath's flock, our service I rejoined,
but mine spirit troubled by Uxbury's dangerous state of mind.
When worship ended I readied limbs to busy rigours chore
spent the aft cleaning, counting down the hours,
sun sets strip bout fifth hour for it still April time,
took mine walk to hammock to rest mine brain a while.

XX

Awoke I to slight shake, Bozeman had appeared,
beckoned I to Quarters for meal time to share,
little didst I realise the Earl's wish use that hour,
to investigate mine past, mine story his explore.
"Jonah, pray tell, of thine heritage please advise,
thine lineage, thine circumstance; be our blessing thine describe,
appear thee a common man yet wisdom doth drip thine lips,
tell us some the history, thine appearance 'pon mine ship."

XXI

"Gentlemen, if tongues bulged at self-reveal most wouldst choke away
but I have spent many years mine ego trying to slay,
for gossip doth add to stories, most enjoy a tale's inflate,
but hope I not given to flatterers ingratiate.
I'll share from broad leaning, I'll speak o this just once,
please then respect for if any talk I'll by quick word circumvent,
if obstacle youse discover I fraid it there to stay,
truth be told I've forgotten most; its deliberately hid away."

XXII

"Lived I midst kings abroad a stately hall,
a prince of north in realm now unnamed,
'pon mine father's head wore he a temporal crown,
by sword o nemesis our kingdom wast struck down.
Strengths vigour vanquished, historys shadow blots our name,
mine brothers, sisters murdered for each they cruelly slain.
Escaped I, ran the countryside, tried the enemy confound,
survived a while but eventually in chains they hadst me bound."

XXIII

"Our nation hated our family for mine father stole and raped,
stripped the poor past nothing, brought indigence their gates,
destitution results in danger for to the east some rebels turned,
cajoled an enemy our slaughter, our wealth their bounty earned.
Executions date sealed mine fate, vengeance for the crowd,
mine neck for blades despatching, mine bones for their dust pound,
loyal soldier aided mine escaping, by night I ran by stealth,
two months I ran scratch feeding, by exhaustion failed mine health."

XXIV

"The angel o death was stalking, mine mortals within his reach,
scythe sharpened ready, this world mine soon release,
but found I then by a farmer, a believing man o faith,
opened to me his hospitality, five years spent then safe.
Found solace tending oxen, planting wheat and corn,
felt liberty... at ease working... tilling God's soil brown,
preached he the gospel message which I drawn to believe,
baptised I then in waters, o all mine sins relieved."

Part 4. Plough the Horizon

XXV

"Agricultural life best suited, saw the seasons change o days,
autumn bright leaf colours, winters snow drift rage,
spring a time of new birth to summers bask o sun,
five years passed I toiling whilst bloodline corroded numb.
The farmer died one spring time, I left his sons and wife,
headed for the port for the business o sea life,
I worked the tides for years at end; know half the discovered world,
skilled at all things nautical and the preaching o His Word."

XXVI

"A Prince and not an Earl," jested Bozeman to the Earl,
repeated his discovery, "a Prince and not an Earl!"
Uxbury raised not to jesting, decided his retort,
"A Prince and not a King!" we laughed to Bozeman's hurt.
I bid mine leave the gentlemen, felt I'd said enough,
both had good manners mine tale their non rebuff
for they wouldst be the last words shared mine pedigree,
ventured to mine hammock to dream atop the seas.

XXVII

Third day from last Sabbath, ten knots off Sicily's coast,
Uxbury signalled his ships, voyage Captains soon aboard,
quarantined to his Quarters o'er charts their supervise,
a route to eastern shoreline for Jerusalem's arrive.
None had ventured past Athens, depths knowledge each denied
and charts canst tell of hidden hell, where rocks lurk to destroy,
stood I adrift at rooms rear their debates I o'er heard,
I waited for Uxbury's sanction afore I shared mine words.

XXVIII

"Ruminations require decision, which I'm charged to mine command,
we not seasoned in these waters, we somewhat guided blind,
we've reached a juncture perilous yet desire I safe return,
I take responsibility the direction we now turn.
A pathway south seems reasonable, Cyrenaica's port Cyrene,
restock our vitals; repair any damage now unforeseen,
to Egypt's Alexandria our fellows short release
then north plough to Jaffa our journey to complete."

XXIX

Officers hale and hearty nodded wide approve
for the Earl locked eyes each Captain then toward me directed look,
enquired mine minds fermenting held his tongue mine secrets reveal,
the Captains' eyes suspicious their doubts not well concealed.
"Seems a plan but I hasten these are much less travelled seas,
most tonnage sails north Cyprus east Pamphylia and Greece.
Most mariners this season consider last of winter's claw
for winds can descend to chaos when mixed with cold freeze raw."

XXX

Endorsement I took from silence, Uxbury's ratification implied,
took I care to explain Mediterranean's April tides,
many ships lost to disaster by sudden storm attack,
another consideration southward the dreads of pirate sack.
"If mine ship I sailing I'd plot course south o Crete,
not too distant Fair Havens where Acts Paul took sanctuary,
and if with good weather blessed then south to Cyrene's port,
but if safety be the measure keep eyes not far from coast."

Part 4. Plough the Horizon 73

XXXI

"Thine counsel ist enlightened: thank you Jonah," voiced the Earl,
turned his charges for decipher, mine words for their confirm,
"Agreed then Captains! Come hither to line our voyage chart,
take observation for each vessel case storm doth chase us part."
The men left their station rowed back to reach their ships,
course set easterly, Syracuse last port lights lit,
bound 'pon adventure, fortyish days give or take,
relished I the prospect of Jerusalem's streets partake.

XXXII

Slow to commence, augury deep growl, omens swell from heave,
from fathoms depth stored below, devil's cauldron found release,
the sky grew grim we eight days in, all hell broke loose the decks,
loud bells to warn, to positions called each soul 'pon four ships.
Of fright a sudden scream of light, thunders roar echoed round,
Uxbury shouted orders, signalled for prayer from tempests harm,
supplication hands I lifted, mine plead to Him on High,
Almighty God please us protect; bless those about to die.

XXXIII

We grouped a huddle ships four in case lives required to save,
flagged colours indicated instructions, bright signals through the waves,
caught the eye of Edwards, strength etched 'pon Bozeman's face,
last I saw of him a while as ship plunged down to depths.
Rose we... creaked the hull... one poor sod flung o'er board,
no use trying to help him lest a dozen more death gored.
Wind paced increased momentum, our sails Uxbury ordered in,
crew tying down all that vital at this the storms begin.

XXXIV

Lantern light drew early dark, vicious waves pillaged deck,
furious clouds unleashed cold ice midst freezing rains and spit,
obsidian patrol of night riders, we lunging, tossed atop,
no starlight calm that even-tide, no moon for directions plot.
Black waters pummelled, pulled more deckhands to dislodge,
men nare seen again, last breaths pulverised from lungs.
Harbingered Uxbury our destruction, steely nerve encouraged mine pleads,
continued I mine worship 'pon gruesome boisterous seas.

XXXV

Daylight hour relinquished dark, second ship sported broken mast,
all others still in tow though damage had harassed,
crews kept busy by the Earl; keep them from thinking his surmise,
injured men limbs twisted tended by surgeon's bloodied knives.
Counted dead, ship lost a score, those decked sewed into shrouds,
cast o'er board to greedy seas, last plunge to graves sea floor,
same each ship I recorded loss, total bout seventy men,
contemplated I their eternities; which place each landed in.

XXXVI

"Cleanse the decks! Cleanse the decks of blood and men's entrails,"
came the charge of Uxbury, "To spare us from disease..."
I clasped a sweep and scrubbed for salt waters toxin release
and thought of Christ's own Blood shed on Calvary's cursed tree.
By post at tiller the Earl was tied, by ropes his hold of grip,
"By all thats right, with all mine might, I'll save my bounty ship!"
Bozeman too for he had reappeared, a bandage bound his head,
tied he too, took position; brave men nay fraid of death.

XXXVII

Night approached, the stiffening storm gathered for a strike,
coiled springs of energy struck with asp of poisons bite,
treacherous scrapes from below yet from deck we spied no rocks,
desperate near, stalking fear took possession each our hearts.
A stretch of moan, compress of wood, thudded gnash of hulls,
small holes punctured, men sweat tended, filled with grease-lined plugs.
Longest night of terror to faint light horizon east,
calming seas releasing slow the tentacles of the beast.

XXXVIII

The loss of a man is heartbreak but that of many birthed numb,
marshalled ships on calming seas, all counted clear but one,
ship the third with her Captain Dare, missing 'pon the waves,
we feared her loss and counted cost, one hundred souls way-laid.
Uxbury stormed the deck in vex, his face red tempered raw,
deep loss he felt but not for men but ships hold for captured ore,
"One quarter's space," he grumbled loud, "The ruination of mine plan!"
I struggled at time to contemplate; his revenge to understand.

XXXIX

Crow's nest signalled our alert to cause,
a faint outline grey appeared, through mist our course applied,
measured plot against the sun, our charts then supervised,
Fair Havens port for anchor drop; vindication in crews eyes.
Two days we laboured at repairs, all hands from dawn to dusk,
late the second the third ship limped and beside us took her berth.
The Earl embraced his Captain mate, elation danced his eyes,
turned to me without one word but cast forewarn his despise.

XL

Two weeks later our depart, Fair Havens the men had enjoyed,
ships well tended, safe repaired; all freshly full supplied,
onward, eastward, toward Jaffa our employ,
excitement building which I couldst nay deny.
From bout tenth day, the bow each morn took me mine standing
to catch first glimpse Judean headland; anticipations joy.
Jerusalem; the mirror of the hearts constructs and contrivances,
where one couldst find their life or perhaps where one might die.

Part Five

Jerusalem...

Built by God... prowled by the devil.

JERUSALEM

aleph

"Who wouldst wish for Heaven, when hell doth such entice!"
accosted Uxbury mine sleep with daggered whisper coarse of voice,
"Be on thine guard Jonah, watch both front and backward eyes
for time willst tell success or fail thine death neath these skies.
I've observed thine venture folly, mine soul thou wish to save,
directing fancy words mine way, mine conscience thou assail.
I'll have mine way Jonah; that fact don't dare forget,
for I'll leave bounty port again with no preacher 'pon mine decks."

beth

Such be the threat of madmen, serpent tongue that conjures bile,
hearts plotting poisons drip slow through life's glass vial,
vengeance be their master; dead in boots devoid of joy,
kanker plaque their chambers beat robbing mortals passing time.
Awoke full to dagger prick, blood flow caught mine neck,
grasped the Earl's lunging wrist, quick turned him flat his seat,
I flung his steel of silver sharp, its collide 'pon the floor
then sat atop olde England's Earl, his eyes ablaze with fire.

gimel

"Legion demons swirl yer brain, Gadarene assault yer ears,
their pitter patter deception, youse been purchased to their hire
but glory to mine Master for strength o lion He gives,
yer calloused heart He forewarned for the Roar o Judah lives.
Revenge plot gainst Henry and youse fraid I stand in way,
whatever reigns yer thoughts I canst decipher brinkmans play,
The Lord rebuke you Jude wrote, to youse I cast same words,
begone Earl o Uxbury; curseth be yer woes."

daleth

Tremble shook his slither frame, the asp of Uxbury winched,
    fear visible his countenance, dread manifold complex,
  by cape of dark he shielded, pulled hood for his disguise,
  slunk back to rooms dark corner with furtive glance his eyes.
Like a ghost his stench depart, smelt his breath mixed mine blood,
    stood to wash mine injury, considered what he'd done,
    not too deep this bruising, razorcut observed by light,
Uxbury had advantaged his authority this fateful pass of night.

hey

Jaffa shore but one day out, all principals called to ship
    to ponder plans for travel train yonder forty clicks,
  they talked, guffawed, ate and drank for voyage near an end,
  close one-third year sailing; tensions ready for disband.
Master Ceremony Uxbury, he played a gracious host,
  raised his glass his gentlemen with vigorous last toast,
  "On to Jerusalem Captains, to Second Baldwin King,
to adventure's tempting and the wealth that it willst bring!"

vav

Portrayed no inkling his attack previous night 'pon mine life,
    as if it mine imagination its trouble and blade strike,
  neck though raw and stinging, hidden cut by coloured scarf,
  he called his men's attention fore each hit their berth.
"One last thing I make mention gents, of this you'll be best pleased,
    we'll take not Jonah with us, I grant not his release,
  for the crew will stay at stations, they'll need his wisdom verse,
six months will be their waiting fore King Henry gains his purse."

zayin

"They'll kill him," roared a Captain, a smile from his stained lips,
"They'll string him up alive and roast him o'er spit."
His mates buoyed with honey mead joined with taunting curse,
Bozeman stood aghast whilst Earl Uxbury raised his toast!
"That ist mine intention fellows; he'll be dead fore city's reach,
him and his disciples, the crew willst burn each piece,
your delight I've seen you've taken, that good news saved till last,
at Jonah now take one last look: his involvement now ist past."

chet

"Mine faith being tested," said I to Edwards who stood at mine aside,
"Fear not Bozeman for I'll ride Jerusalem seated at Earl's right,
Jerusalem mine destiny, the city's title I heard twice,
for torment willst scald Uxbury fore passage o this night."
Bozeman stood mouth open, words trapped and well concealed,
I'm sure he thought us crazy; two fools mad diseased.
"Bozeman; Abraham said to Isaac whilst considering the promise of I AM,
watch and see our delivery; The Lord's provision o a ram."

teth

Twenty four hours our last encounter Uxbury staggered mine side,
fear and wax face laboured like pale terror of nightmare's child,
"Jonah! A devil! It charged mine scythe to reap,
white metal scald, dragged me down to Hades' bleakest keep,
a bastion of monsters, demon shrieks of vile,
tied me... chained in irons... detained me this long time.
Jonah... Jonah... Whats the mean of this?
Am I damned of all men or willst He gift release?"

yod

"If we plotted further north Damascus be in sights,
where Saul bathed in murder observed The Lord in light,
repented Saul o works and deeds, his ambitions changed forthwith,
o youse though I worried Earl for the devil has his grip!
Youse heard repents call oft before, indeed youse I called by name,
I fear The Lord hast gifted vision yer futures roast by flame!"
He cried a river dry that night yet his heart remained untouched,
requested mine accompaniment, tones apologetic red with blush.

yod-aleph

The Captains mumbled mutinous groan the rising of fresh morn
for stood I there at Jaffa's quay in uniform adorned,
the Earl stared each man down, one by one their nod comply
whilst Edwards slapped with pat mine back a glint from his wink eye.
Jaffa a busy crusade port, we harnessed equipment midst much noise,
one hundred men our army, caravan loaded with supplies,
commissions uniform each dressed with shine of armour bright,
flag flutter catching breeze upon the ports alight.

yod-beth

Industry saturated Jaffa's city, her towers and walled surround,
agents buying… selling… languages unique of sound,
we exited the city boundary to a route of dust beat track
soldiers at the ready to combat veiled attack.
Odd sights this road of plenty, nomadic wheels of trade,
shuffling groups with baggage, sacks filled with spice and grains,
camels too, strange roaming beasts, humps encased with crates,
tribes vying for quayside barter and terms advantage for their freight.

yod-gimel

Oasis pools for May-time cool, gave horses our dismount,
watered beasts and gave them rest, shades import paramount,
citrus juice from peculiar fruits pumped sugars through our blood,
half a day we wiled away shielding skins from midday brunt.
Bozeman beckoned me to stroll, enquired Earl's change of mind,
expected he mine slaughter and not sharing of these miles,
told Bozeman of flames visit, repentances offer of console,
reinforced The Lord's mercy and His sovereign control.

yod-daleth

Five miles our destination, first glimpse of rebuilt wall,
even-tide's mist gathering, o'er city drenched its pall,
a signal our diversion, a deviation from our path,
crusader castle, a cousin of Earl, our lodging for the night.
Our arrival expected, tables full for hungers tease,
musicians string of instrument, chords harmoniously expertised,
Bozeman bid me to the stage with licence from our host,
tale of olde to tell again to bring life to times past lost.

yod-hey

"Jerusalem always o intrigue, but a tale more recent times,
four decades ago by Egyptians the city their reside,
Urban Pope his Crusade heralded, the city liberate,
called he foreign Knights to arms; Jerusalem emancipate!
To the Holy Land for unholy task Urban seduced his mob,
his reward, a grant dispensation, indulgences from above,
close one hundred thousand answered, armed with sword and bow
travelled to the region by overland and boat."

yod-vav

"Last year o last century the hordes made their play,
imagine... those seeking God's peace went to kill and slay,
thou shalt not kill forgotten, they released to murderous intent,
barbarity ordered like Herod to kill those innocent.
Those villainous and debauched, those who loved blood to spill,
poured together into Jerusalem to satiate their fill,
found they the region divided, the enemy by faction split,
division over-ruled solidarity yet surrenders terms not writ."

yod-zayin

"Battle paints romantic, hero poised 'pon a steed,
rearing hind leg quarters, sword flash iron clean,
drums and beat o cymbal, impress o trumpet call,
sell yer soul to madness, to yer sacrifice; yer fall.
Forgotten in heat o carnage, a lady's wait at home,
children round a hearth place, coals dimmed quick from warm,
no news o Knight's death parting, no tale from bloody trail,
memories eventually fading leaving etch 'pon some cold grave."

yod-chet

"Pon a broken hill, gallant knight by danger slew,
succumbed his wounds slowly, observed vultures circling low,
grown men around him, adrenaline thrusting their attack,
drag and clank of armour; no surrender... no turn back.
He watched... detached... blood slowing,
skin crept a pallor pale,
this same black bruised mountain
where Christ was shod by nail."

Part 5. Jerusalem

yod-teth

"Death or Victory – Urban's motto call from Rome,
ironic when one considers he safely tucked at home,
mayhem in the city, defenders retreated to Temple Mount,
Saracens for a time safe, protecting Al-Aqsa mosque.
The city fell that summer, Duke Godfrey given power,
his reign confirmed by Crusaders though very short his hour,
Urban sent emissary Daimbert, forced Godfrey Jerusalem's cede,
plus the port o Jaffa giving Rome dominion o'er seas."

keph

"Crusade states by four were named, lands that stretch from south,
borders port o Eilat to Taurus Mountains north,
Principality o Antioch, Counties Edessa and Tripoli,
The Kingdom o Jerusalem found west o Syrie.
Now known this land called Outremer, another jostling name,
for history books record notes o titles oft changed,
Canaan, Philistia, empires Babylon to Rome,
Jacob named Israel by Yahweh; the Holy Land o olde."

keph-aleph

"Godfrey went the way of dust, relinquished he his bones,
crusade knights to Edessa to find a king for throne,
Baldwin, brother Godfrey, succumbed to tempters quest,
he accepted coronations objective; the Levant's enemies to oppress.
Attrition his speciality, war o grandest stage,
the destruction o Egypt became his act to play,
beguiled he political divisions, historical rivalries he enflamed,
conquered he the coastlands and took his bribes from trade."

keph-beth

"Apart the hearts His children there is a city of Yahweh's doting,
that municipality be Jerusalem, Baldwin II now her king,
Jerusalem, created and nurtured, crushed at times by Yahweh
ist prowled by the devil; serpent seed his wish to build.
Celestial reflection is Yahweh's final promise
but satan spins his spindle web o lies and false deceit,
Baldwin II has brought stability, peace to turmoil's region,
beware however the morrow and the marching o our feet!"

keph-gimel

Left I the evening soiree, I left the noise behind,
took mine steps the garden and fertile planted vines,
olive trees olde standing, here from time of Christ,
fruitful still their harvest, rich oils seasoning in casks.
All quiet and resting listless, a serenade from hunting owl,
bleating of some distant sheep, their echo blast off ground,
The Lord had promised mine path here, by faith didst best believe,
by His grace He delivered me; His love and great mercy.

keph-daleth

Bozeman came after time pass, sat silent mine aside,
drank in surrounding landscape and starlight twinkling bright,
relayed reception mine tale tell, witnessed to awkwardness abound:
How didst I possess such knowledge? Who gifted insights found?
Compared mine friend to Nicodemus, the Pharisee visitor of night,
struggling with his conscience, seeking answers from on High,
encouraged him to consider, kingdoms of Heaven and of earth,
that prayerfulness in Jerusalem could gift him too new birth.

keph-hey

I rode at the rear to scrutinize Jerusalem's city,
mine eyes cast toward sun and its east burning rise,
polished troop helmets, spear mounted, flags flying,
five miles to travel from our castle grounds outlie.
Five miles our progress to the city of David,
road busy with labourers, to walls for their wage,
ramshackle carts sporting slab and sand mixing,
rolled crooked rocking forward from outposts far away.

keph-vav

From three miles out a heightened discerning,
build block of brick towers with defences her surround,
white stone, brushed lime, rising and falling,
men shaping placements, stones moved by wooden boughs.
Outside strewn with the dislodge of previous empires,
I imagined the conquests and shouts of battle roar,
granite huge, the shielding of protection,
entry gates visible, I felt at last at home.

keph-zayin

Distant rumbling, the noise of the city,
I stopped... looked east... the Mount of Olives arose,
littered tombstones, sepulchres white baking,
the sun broke the hilltop like Christ's soon return.
Below valley Kidron, garden Gethsemane,
I bowed mine head, a tear it didst fall,
sat I silent... thankful prayer praising,
o'erwhelm of emotion; o'erload of enthral.

keph-chet

Eyes northward the campground of Crusaders,
tents lining part this ground from this century's turn,
close the tomb given by Arimathea,
that tomb found empty; by resurrection Jesus Christ raised full form.
That past time of sins reconciling,
stripped bare to a tree, one would think men should learn,
Christ Jesus Almighty, only Begotten of The Father,
continues to this day by men their Saviour spurn.

keph-teth

Tending south-west the Gate of David,
our entry point Jerusalem, passed under dome of stone,
David, warrior and forgiven sinner,
slayer of goliath whose head fell off by sword.
David, the voices praised by ten thousands,
after Saul he anointed king with power,
friend of God and leader of the nation,
commemorated to the right; fortification of his tower.

lamed

South the tower we dismounted our party,
organised our bearings, Uxbury's battle line was drawn,
we'd march the streets toward Baldwin's palace,
The Temple of Solomon, same high ground as Dome.
Like a Centurion, the Earl placed his soldiers,
steady pace to boot step prompting echo sounds,
the Earl knew Baldwin wouldst be waiting,
sentry wouldst have recognised flag bear of Henry's crown.

lamed-aleph

"Create the theatre Bozeman," smirked our leader.
"By coloured flags of London and metal clank of sound,
armed but in keep with peace time,
Baldwin willst us welcome like a brother kin of arms."
"But we'll terrify the city," remarked Bozeman Edwards.
"They'll hurry all to hiding fraid we'll slay!"
"Indeed," agreed Earl Uxbury fore laughing,
"That is the very essence of this our mock charade!"

lamed-beth

It not mine expectation that I wouldst meet the King,
thought Uxbury wouldst leave me with his troop,
so I took to thorough-fares meander
for I not commissioned under Henry's military oath.
Forced mineself to rear, some time to call mine own,
stepped down the Street of David passing stalls and homes,
shouts of bazaar vendors, passing scents of cooking meats,
wished mine stay forever to dwell these fabled streets.

lamed-gimel

The neigh one horse disturbed me,
glare of sun, I lifted hand to brow,
Uxbury above me, his stallion bucked at will.
"Jonah in Jerusalem," his taunt with menace thrill,
"I knew I'd find you at slow pace, taking sights to quench thine fill,
I'll have no dawdling deserters, join us if thou willst!"
"Earl believe me when I say it, I'll take mine walk pace time,
King Baldwin won't see youse immediately; yer entry he'll deny!"

lamed-daleth

"Nonsense," the Earl retorted. "Knowest thou not thine talk,
letters possession we enjoy under the Seal of England's Host."
I smiled akin a husband placating a wife's maddened growl,
"Mine poor man... When didst a King ever defer to an Earl?"
Stunned was Uxbury, his speech all but spent
yet cast he foulest curse midst words most violent.
"Youse'll feel at home here Uxbury where yer devil tempted The Lord,"
last words from gallop hooves the Earl from saddle heard.

lamed-hey

Left at crossroad turning, street Saint Stephen long,
martyr the first, he wast gifted death by stone,
narrow right, drew a labyrinth warren,
covered shadowed streets encased like tombs.
Children ran and scampered, cajoled for pass of coin,
women weary laboured, tried seduce me them to join.
Harken then a courtyard, surround by shielding brick,
Church of the Holy Sepulchre stilled mine vision fixed.

lamed-vav

Construction work continues this piece of city ground,
they say this here where Christ Almighty died,
nailed by Romans; crowned by thorn.
This day it boasts an army,
black clad widows clothed like crows,
petitioning Yahweh's blessing; Jerusalem's sanctuary from foe.
I prayed mine Father's will, I prayed mine soon release,
with reverential bow resumed explore of zigzag streets.

Part 5. Jerusalem

lamed-zayin

Colours, scents, imagination... stand sell hawkers trading calls,
Nomadic Bedouin, European militia, Englishe and the Gaul,
exotic imperfections, busy dialogue,
Baldwin the city had opened winning respect from factions all.
The cradle of humanity, Levantine fertile plains,
history and commerce, freemen; rich and slave.
Yahweh's brewing concoction, a heady flavoured mix,
at peace a time forgiving yet never far from brandished sticks.

lamed-chet

Via Dolorosa, suffering sorrow once His walk,
plied a cross beam shoulders, scarred and whipped to bones,
His business free atonement, Blood release of slave,
believers to servant-hood instructed, to follow narrow way.
I trampled the beaten pathway, by time stones smoothed round,
care needed in times rainfall lest like Jesus one fell ground,
walls tall to Mount Moriah, a large expanse of city map,
once flattened by siege Titus, not one stone left intact.

lamed-teth

Steps by sunshine yellowed, a rise to plateau plain,
slabs of footstep granite, weeds sprouting in the grain,
dome of centuries standing, the whole city its survey,
walls sharp to incline, octagonal in shape.
This Mount a place for pilgrims,
their assault the skies with prayers,
some seeking restitution
others salvation from The Lord.

mem

Down further right the palace, built stout impose of tower,
include of Templar's portion, home to King's Knights proud,
    a hive and den of iniquity, intrigues swell of mix,
    this place of royal engagement and play of politic.
One hundred men in chain mail, slow cooked sizzling burnt,
    frustrated standing silent, stewed in midday brunt.
    Uxbury turned and saw me, his temper tried he still,
for Baldwin had denied entry; appointments somewhat filled!

Part Six

The Seed of Historie Future...

*All contemporary events are shaped
by the cunning of antecedents dead.*

THE SEED OF HISTORIE FUTURE

aleph

"Of all the dogs under heaven, we found an insolent cur,
pursuing his politic of hindrance," Uxbury spat in slur,
"Mine covenant be with royal London and Rome's ruling Popes,
in the authority of three I stand: is mission devoid of hope?
No accede to meeting, no deference extend toward request,
closed door, thrice bolted; I to be summoned at Baldwin's behest."
With rabid bite of snarl unleashed the Earl battle lined his men,
yet birthed sense his temper quell to compose formalities again.

beth

"If it please," interjected Bozeman, "The men by heat half dead,
for armour bathes a cauldron, strength hast ebbed like lead,
please sire, to the castle, despatch thine swelter rank of troop
and I willst petition Baldwin, fore later our regroup.
Let Jonah take record of witness for he deft with parchment scratch,
let civility strike her bargain versus spurious attack
for if Baldwin hunts thee by Templar thine odyssey willst be doomed;
there'll be no return to Henry with thine legacy surely ruined."

gimel

And so the force disbanded, to castle five miles didst go,
pace slower than morning with shouldered heads stooped low,
Baldwin correct to express umbrage to subversive's threat unfound,
the Earl in plot misguided limped home to lick his wounds.
Discarded we our armour, our belts of long sword broad,
sat in under garments, in shade by shadowed wall,
reverential our disposition, humility of intention best portrayed,
long our talk hours passing; for wisdom we both prayed.

daleth

Bozeman was close to Christ committing,
largely aware his sinful life,
fraid though the opinion of others,
the reaction of his wife.
I continued his encourage,
knowing only The Lord couldst draw him near,
for salvation by grace alone is gifted
'pon surrender in repentant fear.

hey

The night drew black across Moriah, faint chink door candlelight,
Templar Knight walked over with extend of King's invite,
offered cloak for respectability fore palace our survey,
we accepted kindly offer and by wash cloths faces bathed.
Not to stately throne room, dining hall or library,
the Knight led us the kitchen, plain table foods arranged.
"Come eat, take thine comfort," Baldwin stood to our amaze,
"We shall talk after nourishment for by heat I'm sure thee drained."

vav

He proceeded to leg fowl guinea, red wine his draft imbibe,
we he joined, slightly nervous, yet to us he seemed inclined.
Mid-fifties swathe of manhood, lined deep from battles waged,
broad dash of virile stronghold, close crop tight of mane.
Husband to dead Morphia, blessed four daughters their arrange,
no stranger to conquests encounter; twice by his enemies jailed.
King a dozen years well tested, a pious man of prayer,
had learnt he a passing pilgrim; that temporary his reign of care.

Part 6. The Seed of Historie Future

zayin

Gifted in oratory, wide breath knowledge his understand,
asked why England's flag emblazoned far from Henry's hand.
Informed we of our travels, engagement too from Rome,
relayed news of Honorius' passing but this fact already known.
Ship repairs had been slower than the passage of bad news,
but on hearing of two Roman Popes he chuckled his amuse.
Three letters sealed hast Earl Uxbury, expeditions mission to confer,
"A canny man," opined Baldwin, "and me just an insolent cur!!"

chet

Winched Bozeman barbs reaction, apology embarrassed to Baldwin,
"What was the man thinking," enquired Jerusalem's King.
"We thought he another invader, for covet most our soil,
realise now intimidation his purpose; that we'd cede to his beguile!
I'll see that fool tomorrow; Edwards depart thee to thine camp,
I'll keep Jonah for assurity lest Uxbury tempted to scrap."
"If it pleases your Highness," with a laugh I tried suppress,
"Methinks the Earl sooner leave me for he wishes oft mine death!"

teth

We walked to door with Bozeman, for depart a horse arranged,
carried he Baldwin's instruction sealed on small sheet page,
Uxbury to arrive in morning, Edwards at his side,
only two of Henry's party; all troops to be left behind.
Any sign of armed forces Baldwin wouldst attack
to consign the Earl to historie and then his four ships sack.
Nodded mine confirm to Bozeman, watched him take his leave,
wondered 'pon Uxbury's reaction; playing both Kings his deceive.

yod

Withdrew we both to kitchen, poured he cups of wine,
sat I for interrogation under gaze his eyes.
"Be not nervous," encouraged Baldwin. "Come drink of cask!"
"Not mine first eventide with royalty," I mustered, "Certainly not last!
Participation at the Lamb's supper, His marriage feast mine hope,
when the true Sovereign o Jerusalem willst rule forevermore.
He sustained life through mine winter, birthed liberty
and drew me here Jerusalem in ship through troubled seas."

yod-aleph

"A believer of some knowledge, opportune this cross of path,"
spoke softly king Baldwin, suspending any threat of wrath,
"Common ground in Christ Jesus, for we share both His grace,
deep mine love for The Lord; Him alone I trust by faith.
I lift to Him mine family, mine children, delight remembered wife,
He mine trust in for guiding realm in times good and seasons strife,
this city and His people, for refreshing and for peace,
His Kingdom willst rest here eventually then wickedness shall cease."

yod-beth

"The majority trust in selves for salvation,
'pon sand their sinking ground,
self-serve ambition their enemy, despising Christ's Blood love.
To idols they pledge allegiance,
carved of wood and precious stone,
trusting dead, dumb, blunt things to ease their conscience home.
Each individual's time is passing, by death each soon be claimed,
relinquish they not pride's fading shadow to trust our Saviour's Name."

yod-gimel

Jerusalem's meander had tempered mine self reliance,
surrender of this life again I gave to The Lord,
transpires first man I spoke with was the King ruling,
breath settled, steeled mine nervous tongue with words.
"It encourages me that youse a believer,
for I wondered through journey what type man youse be,
many King's characters are described in scripture,
some brushed with grace goodly but most deemed ugly."

yod-daleth

"Hosea spoke o judgement, corrupt o northern kings,
their adulterous wage earned hastened Assyrians,
Deuteronomy laid bare, release o curse and dying,
ravaged the population by dart and arrow flying.
Yahweh pruned the unfruitful, cut off thorny boughs,
all corrupt to a man the seat o rule wast found.
Intrigues malfease the creep unease, steps from foreign border,
a wasteland left debauched by prophesised grim slaughter."

yod-hey

"Sin's perpetration feasted 'pon children,
a lost generation sacrificed to fire,
for the stomach o molech growl prowled the heathen,
unleashing campaigns terror straight from hells door.
Judah in south… well… they followed later,
Nebuchadnezzar's Babylon their purveyor o death,
fore the fray midst decay and cob-webbed raze by pillage
a number o great Kings ruled the state protecting town and village."

yod-vav

"Chosen by God for a time of rich blessing,
Asa, Jehoshaphat, forty years Joash,
Amaziah, Azariah, but they left the pagan high places,
Jotham, Hezekiah who welcomed Babylonian envoys east.
Blasting trumpet off Jerusalem's walls to loud crescendo echo,
notes high and mighty, praise to the King,
killed at Megiddo battle by Egypt's Pharaoh Necho,
for last righteous King Josiah the toll bell didst ring."

yod-zayin

"So what kind o King be youse Sire Baldwin?
What kind o King? Peaceful or by lust held sway?
These days youse willst be sore tested
for Henry and Uxbury have youse in sights as prey!"
"Thou knowest thine Kings and historie," mused the sovereign,
"Serious this role from God the part I play.
Historie willst write me mine own epitaph Jonah,
now rest preacher: gather strength for the morrow's swordless fray."

yod-chet

The voice of politic is by crookery tainted,
painted by sweet words with hate infused eyes,
the next morn the Earl sprouted flowery peace make offerings
yet his voice dripped cold, flavoured sour by ice.
By three sealed letters his obsequious request,
"Henry looking to bolster defences; consideration agreed by Rome,
toll collection, to Crown a small percentage,
four full ships necessitated. three of silver, one of gold."

Part 6. The Seed of Historie Future

yod-teth

"I know thine Henry, his reputation haunting,
as I suspected mammon thine intent,
lucre dishonourable, the Crown by covet tempted,
building his fiefdom by measure of stealth!"
"Not in the least," responded Uxbury,
"Sire, cast thine regard o'er these sealed parchments,
for Rome hast agreed herein to King Henry's solicitation,
to this royal engagement their Crusader army lent."

keph

"Rome! That coven of witch stink,
from their temple of plunder they stalk Holy ground,
Rome! Nero's offspring; a cauldron of devils,
multiplied by twosome, now Honorius gone."
"Surely Sire," bowed low Earl Uxbury,
"Rome holds thine future; salvations reward."
"Not so Uxbury," scowled the King of Jerusalem,
"That right belongs to Christ... to Jesus alone."

keph-aleph

All empires be destroyed from strife internal,
even Alexander bequeathed plotting generals four,
at least with an enemy of foreign boot marching,
they'll stare your face full, fore transacting their war.
Not so with Henry, the Earl and two vultures,
ostentatious their scraping, obsequious their bow,
salutations deceiving with lips smiling merry,
they'll strip you of caution then feast off your bones.

keph-beth

After struggle debate the King appraised Uxbury,
hand to mouth pondering, distilling his thoughts,
"Let me study the letters and consider thine statements,
return thine estate; we'll reconvene in the morn."
"If it pleases your Majesty, I'll leave with you Bozeman,
case thou require clarification or... lest parchments are burnt."
"By The Lord mine integrity, thou question mine nature?
How dare thou insult! Begone to thine home"

keph-gimel

We accompanied the Earl outside for his departure,
saddled his steed, from high perch he looked down,
he reminded us both wherein lay allegiances,
firstly loyalty to him fore fidelity the Crown.
"Not an easy adversary Jerusalem's leader,
I can see proficiency in both negotiation and charm,
born leader of men, astute his behaviour
I'll plot best strategy to circumvent impends harm."

keph-daleth

Bozeman and I took up our wait station,
King Baldwin unfolded three embossed scrolls,
studied for hours under remaining warmth sunlight,
ruminating... pausing... marking his notes.
Sat later for mealtime where we met Princess Melisende,
talk of adventure and past histories,
post our meal Baldwin attired long in black garb,
ventured alone, disappeared to the streets.

keph-hey

Bozeman thought it unusual, a King leave his palace,
to parade dark the warrens of streets all alone,
Melisende realised Edwards left guessing,
spoke soft words assuring; allaying alarm.
I encouraged mine friend a walk in the night air,
down steps from Moriah we ambled at ease,
tracing the days, recounting conversations,
wondering how Earl Uxbury planned to surprise.

keph-vav

Cobbled junctions, shadows of Templars,
Knights in black armour by Baldwin arranged,
to protect his path or combat subterfuge of Uxbury,
citizens sequestered; curfewed for night.
Narrow paths, no illuminated bright candles,
the city ourselves, to walls we took step,
out past the gates tented villages and bonfires,
those camping oblivious to potential of threats.

keph-zayin

A beautiful morn, day fore the Sabbath,
we entered the hall the King to converse,
stood Baldwin with a party of Saracen,
men sculpted nomadic; fierce looks of coerce.
Tall striking threesome, bearded, fine linens,
robed in colours to signify tribes,
luscious blues, reds, white robes long flowing,
stood to debate Uxbury's despise.

keph-chet

"An open border, an open city,
only way to end the battles we wage,
for war hast scarred, hast left wounds long suffer,
discussions necessitate mine Saracen friends.
Your quest toll percentage willst extract from those passing,
from mostly the poor, their travail for survive,
labours penny-pinch, they believe act defiant,
willst soon end the peace that mine throne works to strive."

keph-teth

For hours they argued to irate faced bad temper,
no concede of objectives throughout the congress,
we took a break, I from writing of record,
fresh air inhale with Bozeman in step.
Outside a boy, aged bout a decade,
charting with chalks and inks of scrolled paint,
he mapping Moriah, inclines and layout,
capturing finely the buildings and gates.

lamed

I applauded his talent, his mastery of detail,
most city now completed he revealed with pride,
his grandfather busy in talks with King Baldwin,
he instructed to capture his artwork outside.
Mine senses gathered, new urgency heightened,
none consider mere boy a spy in the camp,
bid him success then we hastened to palace;
Babylonian envoys mapping future threat to the peace!

lamed-aleph

Straight to talks where they danced to lips hotly,
Saracens demanded covenant everlast,
Baldwin surprised, had not guessed this pressing
redirected the meeting toward Henry's impasse.
"Henry like Pharaoh of olde, mammon from poor his intent,
gold, land, people taken; driven to slavery by stealth.
Diminish the man; reduced to mud brick his employ,"
He paused… pointed, "Henry wills our Kingdom's destroy."

lamed-beth

"Pure our hearts," scorned Uxbury, "Pure our voyage reveal,
we as men all trustable; nothing left concealed!"
The King interrupted, with bellow of voice laughed loud,
"Pure of heart!
Trustable!
One anyway, perhaps another's half!
Thou art a canny deceiver Earl Uxbury,
drowning in Henry's clasp!"

lamed-gimel

With caution Baldwin turned to the Saracens,
more chosen his words, careful in craft,
"What do you require gentlemen; thine engage with Henry?
Mammon? Water rights? Advise please if thou canst!"
The older man stood stately,
leaned to a gracious stooped bow,
"If it pleases King Baldwin, a covenant.
Land! Specifically our rights to this Mount."

lamed-daleth

Like a blow to the chest with an arrow,
King Baldwin couldst not hide recoil,
backfired his strategy of engagement,
from flank left his negotiations spoiled.
"Agreed to thine request!" rushed Earl Uxbury
but King Baldwin arose fuming raw,
"Of all the low forms I've encountered,
I've experienced naught like thine mutinous charge."

lamed-hey

"I am the King this dominion, this land The Lord's that I reign,
nare fore throughout histories custom hast a King been such enraged.
Uxbury, thou art proven a mercenary
if here resident I'd extract treason's charge,
as for thee Saracen warriors, thine request I dishonourably purge.
I close now these informal discussions
time now to cease this charade,
depart thine respective lodgings, with peace I send all away."

lamed-vav

Baldwin wast wary all factions, stage managed his depart escape,
mine accompany to administer meeting; minutes chore of task.
Asked if I trusted Uxbury, revealed I the truth his wife,
Henry in league with the devil; hold of threat o'er Earl's life.
"The Earl hast seen where he's going, seen it from afar,
torments abode, flesh burning; stench o sulphurous char.
He's up to something your Highness, play o hand I not sure,
vengeance sworn gainst Henry; his intention far from pure."

Part 6. The Seed of Historie Future

lamed-zayin

"Sire, the seed o historie future youse planted,
for outside a Saracen lad,
mapping by subterfuge the city, each warren stone cut o path.
Methinks he an innocent party, he entrusted by that statesman olde,
beware price envoy's welcome and honesty veneered in mould."
"This juncture Jonah not the worry yet after mine death they'll come,
some decades soon our reckon at hand these men's grandsons;
Jerusalem's future willst be blighted; by enemy o'er-run."

lamed-chet

'Pon a Sabbath morn, the bell of Kirk didst peal,
all guilty called to examine the wages of sin for their deeds,
Preacher commissioned to ministry, seeking nay favour nor friend,
if truthful The Word's exposition consciences soon be cleansed.
That Sabbath I asked to expound, God's Word for family of King,
there in the shadow of Calvary, the Cross, the streets where He fell.
All by grace our thanksgiving, to Christ sinners reconciled,
lifting with praise our Saviour; His Blood by faith undefiled.

lamed-teth

Sat tall Destrier high, epaulettes, medals; full war attired,
Earl Uxbury stormed the palace; enraged the King's enthral.
"Thine vision Baldwin ist one people, one city and one King,
but a house divided shall not stand, for trouble it willst bring.
Knights Hospitaller the Pope's legion, by strength of force their camp,
are given to mine authority with legal seal of stamp,
outnumber they thine Templars, I'll order irons strike,
I'll vanquish quickly thine Kingdom; eviscerate its memory o'ernight."

mem

"A brave noble gent, once fraid to die," admonished I Earl Uxbury who vexed in countenance countered not, but diverted quick his eye.
"Haman himself!" interjected the King. "Released a time from fire, demons continue with relished zeal to stoke thine funeral pyre.
Away to thine devilries, straight from hell foulest scourge of fiend, away you devil with poisonous words, extract thine temporary end.
But Earl, remembest thou, carry to thine dying breath...
The Almighty, in His chosen city ist a faithful participant."

Part Seven

Convergence...

Alas! All must soon die... Including you.
Yes! Most assuredly... Including you.

CONVERGENCE

aleph

June doth birth the promise of hotting summer sun,
nature's abundance, vine's mirth sumptuously finely spun,
birdsong eventide echo, clear waters mirrored fresh,
pastures kine full lowing, fragrant blooms; decadently dressed.
Rag-a-tag childs playing, sleep time stretched out long,
merrybow micklebarrow morris dance to dulcet toots of horn.
Solstice month of roses that year wore shrouds of black
for that summer Uxbury birthed forth the putrid stench of death.

beth

From stallion steed of muscle strap Baldwin called me his aside,
five miles clandestine canter, Uxbury's castle distant spied,
demanded the Earl's presence, me thoughts admonishment,
but lo! The heart of Baldwin wast brought to covets test.
One-third the treasure collected the King's price for comply,
this bribe wouldst guarantee Templars to Henry's mission guide,
the Earl speechless wavered, negotiations glint his eye,
percentages for the reckon with throwing of the die.

gimel

"baal's disciple and Jezebel," with tear of voice I cried,
"For youse Baldwin I thought perfect, mine faith in men restored,
proud mine beating breast, yer aside mine time adored.
Knowest I that Ux a danger, the type to blade one's back,
one to smile upfrontly while plotting his attack.
Foolish mine endeavour taking comfort yer reside,
yet covets work ist ceaseless, it births adultery's bride.
For the gallows yer both worthy to hang from bough rot high."

daleth

One thousand mile by three through vale and mountain pass,
rivers, lakes and forests, pilgrims tiring on their path.
Jerusalem to London, every hamlet in the tween,
yet all royal mortals by mammon hearts deceived.
King Baldwin expressed his anger yet Uxbury feigned non care,
failed to strike their bargain, then cocked to trigger hair,
spat the ground brown mudding, Baldwin waved dismiss,
repentance urged I strongly as hooves the ground force bit.

hey

Mammon be a lure to moral degradation,
please heed warn near completion, the telling of mine tale.
A golden calf the Hebrews worshipped in the desert
constructed from their trinkets forged in fires bright flame,
hearts purchased to dissention, miracles forgotten, abandoned quick,
Commandments Ten by Moses smashed in pieces thick.
Mammon's disease plunders, brings death, to hearts a callous,
rich men dying whilst building larger barns.

vav

Stationed I with Uxbury who in final preparation,
despatching tax collectors, trade routes north and south,
ports of bill goods lading, Jaffa, Caesarea,
strategic points of interest; borders fat and large.
Hospitaller and troops of Henry provided paid surveillance,
weapons readied, steadied, to siphon passage toll,
long nights spent subversively, imagining potential taxes,
nothing to escape Henry's maddened grip of claw.

zayin

Traders herded to extractions brutal quarter,
to enter marketplace one had to pay the toll,
no buying, no selling without licensed stamp of record,
antichrists well versed in tightening power lust laws.
Tolls in form of coinage preferred by tax collectors,
though crops and beasts too taken; later by Earl sold.
Then under cover darkness funds to Henry's coffers,
all stolen from citizenry wast converted to precious ore.

chet

It took two months to bite, the effects of price inflation,
merchandise margins tight left the public wallet stung,
commodities became sparse as trading slowed to snail pace,
for to town market centres the farmers did not come.
The black-market flourish gained with the selling of illegal,
the nation blamed King Baldwin for hungers belly tight.
Commerce almost ceased while merchants loudly grumbled,
looked for foul of means solution to force an end their plight.

teth

Townsfolk's banded into groups civilian angry,
with clubs and implements they lay in patient wait,
surrounded night-time convoys of Uxbury's nefarious pillage
and plundered the contents to share in midst their grief.
Baldwin restored his dignity and pointed to the foreigner,
by unelected heathen, fifth column country sacked,
across the nation the people rose in union
fore Earl Uxbury regrouped to unleash hell's attack.

yod

Piles of dead left wafting in the heat of sun tall burning,
penalty extracted from innocents with a price oft paid in blood,
striking Hospitaller sorties, under flags of Rome,
men with cross-bowed arrows slaying young and olde.
This world takes shape peculiar when agendas are appalling,
national sovereignty over-ruled, human rights denied,
same through every race, beginning to times ending,
till Christ again one day returns bringing evil it's suspend.

yod-aleph

Curved to bend and leather fastened, strike of terror, sharpened blade,
Scimitar swords defend from Saracen's East Brigade,
spice route raised they plied their trade by crimson thrusts unsheathe,
extracting grains and bounty meats securing sought relief.
Desert raids by Saracen blades, by sand dune dark night crawl,
backed secretly by Baldwin who wished King Henry's fall.
Hospitaller Order took full brunt losing several hundred men
but Henry's guerrillas continued to rob by close re-work their plan.

yod-beth

On one such raid a price was paid for Bozeman he was hurt,
an arrow bolt came hurtling and struck him chest full brunt,
broken collar, twist of neck and bleed from his left ear,
unconscious full o'ernight his drift tween heaven and here.
To Jerusalem for quackery, the cut of surgeon's knife,
who with great care undertook the saving of his life.
So the days wiled away, the fleecing toll extract,
reserves quietly building whilst in fray much blood wast spilt.

yod-gimel

Baa Baa Earl Uxbury, hast thou any ore?
Yes Sire! Yes Sire! Three boat loads!
Silver shapes of clipped bits,
coins of golden stored,
refined and smelted slowly,
then shaped in fat fist bars.
By commence September, mission near complete,
saw Uxbury devise his plan for release of Merchant Fleet.

yod-daleth

Captain Dare of olde time, he of ship the third,
sent back to coastlands, to Jaffa's quays of port,
to ready the ship's holding, convert to shelves for load,
to balance weights important ensuring safe for float.
No requirement for equine boarding, for they wouldst not return,
instead exchange for fair price, use earnings for crew's food.
"Get us seaworthy Captain, the men ready for the seas,
implement regimen fitness for the crew hast been at ease."

yod-hey

Harbinger! Mine second insight given to Earl Uxbury,
who sidled up mine nearside seeking an apology.
"The world is full o devils; they seduce to fowler's lair,
malevolent darkened forces seeking hosts to snare.
Stalk and skulk, stab and stamp, they sift living corpses,
thirty round pieces silver stamped with Caesar's name.
Youse think youse not so bad Earl but yer sin is slowly killing,
and a narcissist will always seek someone else to blame!"

yod-vav

"Cage him! Starve him! Beat him! Kill him!"
At the Earl's command I put in chains.
"I deduce," I said, "We not given to kinship,
but mine words o truth youse'll nare escape."
From northern territory a week's cage roll to the castle,
with sun beating down and cold chill at night,
like previous sail on mine plank I wretched, tired and hungry,
perhaps as advised I should silent learn mine voice!

yod-zayin

Near the fort we were set 'pon by Templars,
within a short time mine full escort wast dead,
released from mine cage, yet still in bondage,
wondering if I known by Knights colour battle-dressed.
Under darkness I brought to Jerusalem,
deposited in a prison for several hours,
tell of mine tale must have been transferred to Baldwin,
for he gave mine freedom and in Jerusalem I housed.

yod-chet

Three days a row the King came to visit,
talking, reminiscing, telling many tales,
some matters of state he sought mine true opinion,
taking assurance that King Henry's theft near complete.
Trouble in the north that he wouldst have to visit,
a daughter there he'd stay at her reside,
asked me for a blessing for his journey's heavy labour,
I took the opportunity to discourse mine third insight.

yod-teth

"They took a crooked tree, roughly sinewed from creation,
knotted, boldly folded, crudely shaped in form,
designed for curseth bodies for death didst stalk its branches,
criminals and a scapegoat slaughtered outside town.
Beaten, kicked and plundered, steadied by nails pounded,
Christ Jesus stretched taut tight, shook each moaning thud,
only Begotten Son o Heaven's Holy Father,
murdered to take sin's penalty through the shedding o His Blood."

keph

"God Almighty rules from Heaven's glory splendour,
Holy, Holy, Holy, His angels sing His side,
we humans by very nature are unrighteously self-deceiving,
require a Mediator; a Husband for the bride.
Not one jot, one tittle law Christ had broken,
perfect, spotless, unblemished; a Saviour for the world,
hanging, hewn and broken by The Father He wast rejected,
the sin and curse o this world soldered to His form."

keph-aleph

"Blood and water mingled, His death paid mine ransom,
lovingly shrouded He wast buried in a grave.
From Arimathea's tomb the third day resurrected,
new life freely given to repentant sinners who believe.
Unmerited, unwarranted, unprecedented favour,
by grace alone through faith in Christ Jesus we are saved.
Today Christ ist alive, sits beside His Father,
He alone is worthy to receive our thankful praise."

keph-beth

"Forgive me Jonah; mine lust and richly wealth of covet,
a guilty man I sit here," King Baldwin near tear eyed.
"I am a mere man, mineself by anger sinful,
ask Christ Himself; true repentance He willst nare deny."
We knelt together, a King and a pauper,
raised our hands to praise The Lord on High.
In disarray Baldwin's kingdom, for Antioch now departing,
embraced we like brothers; at peace in Jesus Christ.

keph-gimel

I watched Baldwin leave with his troop of Knightly Templars,
red cross emblazoned on white shields and robe,
to the hospital mine leave to check in with Bozeman,
found the Earl at his bed; under shadows he had come.
Bozeman had recovered, had received new instruction,
by roads o'er land he to London and to Rome,
a letter in his hand, mission summary for Henry,
the bullion now collected; the mission set for home.

keph-daleth

"Why by land?" I questioned Earl Uxbury,
"Simple Jonah," came his curt reply.
"Firstly we might sink and all aboard may perish,
secondly bad storms might havoc our employ.
Good chance storms given it's a close run to year end,
we may require Fair Havens safe of port again.
If by elements affected we might not sail till spring time,
and o'er land willst ensure that Bozeman can explain."

keph-hey

"Mine ships to leave October, giving Edwards some head-starting,
our sail normally two months to Rome,
however, extra weight willst require delicate deliberation
I reckon nearer three till the Pope's gold lands his home.
We'll miss new year in England, it willst add to Henry's frustration,
he'll be pleased though to count whats been stashed in the hold.
Bozeman stay with Aymeric, we'll meet fore years break shortly,
embarkation then at Civitavecchia; destination London town."

keph-vav

Like a rodent chased by children, Uxbury fled the city,
robed in cape with darting scan of eyes,
feet paced to corners, sniffing fore move onwards,
furtive his slither past gate to open skies.
We laughed at the King's Earl, he of noble station,
then agreed to meet the morrow our good-bye.
As I walked I troubled by the instructions given Bozeman;
all too neat and tidy; all perfectly aligned!

keph-zayin

At times of great sadness I miss mine family,
brothers, father, sister and little known mine wife,
so it was next morning, tinged with heart near broken,
farewell to bid mine friend in enemy's camp.
Bozeman Edwards, he a friend best standing
wouldst leave this day with seal of letters stamped.
I walked toward the castle but outside walls he waiting,
two horses tethered together; standing flanked.

keph-chet

"I willst trust Him for eternity," he remarked at our embracing,
"I know I need a Saviour for this a sinful life."
Encouraged by discernment we cantered to the Jordan
where I baptised a brother; born again in Blood bought faith.
Two heavily armed guards his companions 'pon his leaving,
I informed him bout mine diary to be left with Melisende,
I wouldst disappear to some informal Judean setting
to live out the remaining days of this temporal fraught life.

keph-teth

Yes I missed mine friend but joyous his salvation,
three weeks I stayed Jerusalem to finalise mine plans.
Third October I wast called by the Earl to visit Jaffa,
wary took mine path but by danger not alarmed.
On approach I saw four ships set 'pon stirring waters,
weighted heavy they drew at depth low Plimsoll charge,
flags stately bearing the realm of Henry's kingdom,
galley-ways close guarded, each ship a squadron armed.

lamed

Quarter's door shut, I stood mine ground outside,
a few nods recognition, but most crew to tasks applied,
regimented order by Captain Dare viciously restored;
that nemesis plague of galleon of whom death wast even scared.
Earl Duplicity cajoled me, to mine back a slap of welcome.
"Jonah! I bear thee no heart's ill-will, set differences aside,
I thank thee for thine company, please... join me port side,
I'd like to brush the slate clean fore depart this days last tide."

lamed-aleph

"To London soon depart, our venture please thine witness,
ships of four to catch tides stiff current breeze,
soon mine wife and legacy, first re-unite in Rome with Bozeman,
I'll be glad to settle homeward, to retire for times of ease.
You expressed a desire to stay here, Jerusalem thou loveth,
some ministry of gospel be thine charge?"
I stood and smiled the Earl, no confirm to his games guessing,
silent... he then busied to the whistle his crew's call.

lamed-beth

The earlier storms had ravaged, crew now bout three hundred,
a few of course had disappeared to serve on summer boats,
Uxbury visited each ship selecting and dividing sailors,
no comfort familiarity for new Captains appointed each ship.
Captain Dare appointed Bozeman's role replacement,
stood attention hawk-eyed the Earl's immediate right,
to the sound his orders disentangle of shore ropes,
confirmation the flotilla wouldst leave this very night.

lamed-gimel

"One of gold, three of silver," the Earl roared in boisterous,
his treasure chests stored neatly, shelved on heavy planks,
to positions the men, Uxbury signing off authority,
spied me on the quayside and joined me a short while.
"Lonely Jonah?... It hast been some adventure,
that day we hooked thee on board seems long ago,
Aymeric and two Popes, Honorius dead and King Baldwin,
battles bloodshed spilling and ships now filled with ore!"

lamed-daleth

"Jonah, thou hast irked me to bile's discomfort drenching,
yet I've considered thine ministry of words,
correct you have been and I'll ask for mine men's blessing,
their salvation 'pon these seas that we charged explore.
Not for me Jonah, for mine character of a swindler,
to covets avarice mine heart designed to hope,
a fine line to walk, The Lord's command far reaching,
obedience ist difficult when lust's greed hast found a hold."

lamed-hey

"Sire, I'm conscious now yer thoughtful deliberations,
yer conscience struck by turmoil heaven sent,
ministered to by the Word o His gracious instruction,
the architect yer doom is simply unbelief.
For the men I trust them to God Almighty,
safety passage Lord, I pray them soon their homes,
yet I'm disturbed Earl Uxbury this long time passing;
willst yer revenge 'pon Henry affect these innocents aboard?"

lamed-vav

"Two thieves, one each side The Lord hung dying,
one that night to Paradise, the other to the flame,
that pit unleashing insurmountable forever suffering,
a place of tempest foul and gnashing teeth o pain.
Choose The Lord Earl, I beseech youse,
no need to spurn free salvation grace,
vengeance might satisfy but it promises eternal damning;
Call sire! Call 'pon Christ's name."

lamed-zayin

"Jonah, I'll not barter mine future for I trust in what I see,
I sculpted for this world and not eternity,
I have time Jonah; I'll repent some juncture later,
alive I now Jonah; not all mine chances spent!"
"Alas Earl," I replied. "Alas all must soon die,
including youse Earl Uxbury, most assuredly even youse.
Repent Sire, for the kingdom o heaven ist at hand."
"We'll see! We'll see!" came response with step to ship from land.

lamed-chet

Day's last hour, a rouse of cheer, anchors raised and locked,
four ships sails, west homeward bound exited the dock,
sailor's climb to crow's nest high, to Jaffa a last look,
this tidy row of ships lined four carrying Uxbury and flock.
Midst smaller boats with fisher nets manoeuvred they group tight,
saw lanterns light erupt to bright, approach the fall of night.
Watched till dots the horizon dropped, disappear o'er line earth's crust,
imaginations figment then confined their memory to dust.

lamed-teth

'Pon Bozeman's steed I gathered speed through sands, shale and rock,
to Jerusalem mine engage, to Princess Melisende for diary drop,
then nomadic trails toward northern lakes, mission mine design,
prayerful answer discerned from The Lord, His path He well defined.
We ate miles, mine thoughts employed to mammon's deceit and curse,
better saved and better poor than rich in court but lost.
City east, Olive Mount, Jerusalem's walled survey,
stopped and praised place His return; last trumpet's herald day.

Teacher,
which is the great commandment in the law?

Jesus said to him,
"You shall love the Lord your God,
with all your heart, with all your soul and with all your mind.
This is the first and great commandment.
And the second is like it:
You shall love your neighbour as yourself.
On these two commandments
hang all the law and the prophets."

(Matthew 22:36-40)

In the temporary absence of mine esteemed father

King Baldwin II

**I, Princess Melisende
heir to the kingdom of Jerusalem
certify and authenticate this diary
and
notarise it affording legal protection under royal seal.**

October 1130 AD

Addendum

**To his Most Excellent Majesty, Henry the First,
King of England and Duke of Normandy.**

Requesting His Majesty's continued forbearance,

I too have studied Jonah's diary and attest to its veracity; it is a truthful and honest capture of each stage our quest. Jonah has proven to be an admirable scribe conveying accuracy in all situations. Please facilitate tales completion.

Three months of heavy travel found me in Rome. Bid a dishonourable welcome from Aymeric; I was arrested and imprisoned for close a full year's quarter. Earl Uxbury, he informed me, had not returned with the negotiated promise.

Early New Year I was called to Aymeric's presence. Brought to the College of Cardinals I was introduced to the sole survivor of the silver ships. This common sailor, William Shire, confirmed mine witness where 'pon I was released. I endeavour to relay the sequence of events as portrayed by Master Shire.

The Earl's command set 'pon seas early October. The ships four ploughed turbulent waters for three weeks fore they fell victim to a Mediterranean storm. During one fateful day in November 1130AD each silver ship sank; all within four hours of each other. The scene, it seems, was utterly deplorable. Crews transferred to their nearest ship until the last vessel held close to two hundred and fifty souls. Most perished as the last ship descended to the depths. It willst surprise you to hear that Earl Uxbury refused to provide life saving assistance.

It is surmised that in the process of readying the expedition for return that the aforementioned Captain Dare applied some measure of liquid solution to the plugs which had been administered during repair work in Fair Havens. The salt water and additional weight combined and said repairs dissolved. This resulted in the sinking of the three silver bearing ships. William Shire and a small number survived fore all others unfortunately succumbed. Master Shire witnessed Earl Uxbury's ship circle the wreckage fore turning due south.

Some of the Earl's crew were thrown o'erboard including Captain Dare who appeared to have been murdered; multiple stabs wounds evidenced on his chest. While it appears that said Captain was an initial co-conspirator he too fell to the iniquitous avarice of the Earl. Our Commander may have suspected some mutinous intent. Those inherently loyal survived; hence his reallocation of crew duties at Jaffa.

Mine opinion is that Earl Uxbury believed his wife to be already murdered by you King Henry and that his legacy wouldst nare 'gain bear testimony to his family name. His conjecture; his own demise at your hands 'pon return to London! His convoy of deception was therefore planned in advance and undertaken for survival. The value of your stolen gold commensurate with his previous country and city holdings. Whilst guilty of heinous crimes, chief amongst which is the murder of hundreds innocent, I conclude he willst commence again elsewhere free from threat of your warrant.

Under Pope Innocent and Aymeric's instruction I returned to Jerusalem. King Baldwin is nearing death; ill from some northern malady. Princess Melisende and her husband willst assume reigning duty. She provided the copy of Jonah's diary and holds the original in trust. Jonah is ministering in a place unknown.

Your Majesty, let me conclude with three points. Firstly vengeance willst be sought at some future date by the Saracens. The consequence of your charade of death willst be extracted in Jerusalem 'pon some future generation. The Crusade ist not near over and willst cost many ten thousands their lives.

Secondly I will not search out Earl Uxbury. Mine legitimate half brother has vanished. Neither willst I return to London for you wouldst murder me. I too have disappeared.

Finally, Jonah wast correct in his deduction. Time passes quickly and soon you too King Henry willst die. You stand at all times a heart beat from oblivion. Therefore; Repent King Henry for the Kingdom of Heaven ist at hand.

Freeman Bozeman Edwards,
Summer 1131AD.

Other books by Redmond Holt

Testimony: Onward toward salvation.

America

Eulogy: Jerusalem 70AD.

dystHOPEia.

Are you inspired to write a book?

Contact

Maurice Wylie Media
Your Inspirational & Christian Book Publisher
Based in Northern Ireland, serving readers worldwide

www.MauriceWylieMedia.com

www.ingramcontent.com/pod-product-compliance
Ingram Content Group UK Ltd.
Pitfield, Milton Keynes, MK11 3LW, UK
UKHW061222180426
11947UKWH00026B/1972